ALLEN BREED SERIES

The Allen Breed Series examines horse and pony breeds from all over the world, using a broad interpretation of what a breed is: whether created by the environment where it originally developed, or by man for a particular purpose: selected for its useful characteristics, or for its appearance, such as colour. It includes all members of the horse family, and breeds with closed or protected stud books as well as breeds and types still developing.

Each book in the Allen Breed Series examines the history and development of the breed, its characteristics and use, and its current position in Britain, together with an overview of the breed in America and worldwide. More difficult issues are also tackled, such as particular problems associated with the breed, and such controversies as the effect of the show ring on working breeds. The breed societies and their role in modern breeding policies are discussed.

BOOKS IN THE SERIES

The Appaloosa
The Fell Pony
The Hanoverian
The Irish Draught
The Mule
The Trakehner

The Hanoverian

Hanoverian mares and foals at an old stud on Wischhafener Sand Island, Lower Elbe.

ALLEN BREED SERIES

The Hanoverian

Christian Freiherr von Stenglin

Translated by
Christina Belton

with additional material by
Deborah Wallin

J. A. Allen
London

British Library Cataloguing in Publication Data
Von Stenglin, Christian Freiherr
  The Hanoverian.
  1. Hanoverian horses, history
  I. Title   II. Hannoveraner. *English*
  636.1

ISBN 0–85131–478–3

First published in Germany in 1983 by Franckh'sche Verlagshandlung, W. Keller & Co., Stuttgart

Published in Great Britain in 1990 by
J. A. Allen & Company Limited,
1 Lower Grosvenor Place, London SW1W 0EL

Editor Elizabeth O'Beirne-Ranelagh
Book production Bill Ireson
Printed in Great Britain by St Edmundsbury Press Limited,
Bury St Edmunds, Suffolk

Contents

Front cover: Photograph by Werner Ernst shows the stallion Wenzel, by Woermann out of a mare by Matador, born 1976 and owned by the Celle state stud. Reserve champion at the DLG show, Munich, 1982. Ridden here by a *Gestütwärter* from Celle in period costume.

Endpapers: Young stallions at the Hunnesrück stallion rearing centre.

Preface

The Hanoverian is one of the group of regional breeds of Northern Europe, and of Germany in particular, which are collectively known as warmbloods. Warmblood breeding in Germany was originally designed to produce both horses for all kinds of military work, and light draught horses for use in agriculture. Almost from the earliest days of organised breeding, the vast majority of breeders were therefore local farmers, using stallions supplied by the local breeding societies or large landowners, and this tradition is still carried on today. Before German unification in 1871, Germany was made up of a number of different states and the locally organised breeding areas under the control of a local breed society reflected this structure. Thus horses bred in the Hanover area became known as Hanoverians, those bred in the Schleswig Holstein area became known as Holsteins, those bred in Westphalia became known as Westphalians and so on. Apart from the adoption of the East Prussian Horse of Trakehner Origin (better known as the Trakehner) as a national breed bred throughout West Germany following the loss of its original homelands to East Germany, Poland and Russia at the end of the Second World War and the subsequent flight of many Trakehner breeders to what is now West Germany, this regional breeding structure, now under the overall control of the *Deutschen Land-wirtschafts-Gesellschaft* or DLG (the German Ministry of Agriculture) still continues today.

Over the last two centuries the Holstein and the Trakehner (named after the Trakehnen Stud in East Prussia) have developed into two very distinct types and breeds. However, the horses from the other breeding areas, such as Oldenburg, Hanover and Westphalia, although different again from the Trakehners and Holsteins, have become very similar to each other and it is often impossible to distinguish a Hanoverian from a Westphalian without examining each individual horse's brand. One reason for this is that over a considerable number of years many regional breed societies have used the same sires, a practice which still continues today, with popular stallions being graded into two, three or even four different stud books. For those used to the pedigrees of 'pure' native breeds, in which no 'outside' blood is allowed, it is also often confusing to discover that a considerable number of these popular stallions are not, in fact, warmbloods themselves. This is because it has always been a recognised policy in warmblood breeding in Germany and else-where regularly to take into the stud books a certain percentage of high quality

1

Thoroughbred, Anglo-Arab and Arab stallions to upgrade and lighten the breeding stock. Once graded into the breeding stud book these stallions add XX to their names if they are Thoroughbreds (e.g. Der Löwe XX), X to their names if they are Anglo-Arabs (e.g. Kurde X) and OX to their names if they are Arabs (e.g. Fetysz OX) to denote their origin in the pedigrees of their progeny. These progeny are then treated as 'purebred' despite their mixed origins, and the word 'partbred' in warmblood breeding is used to describe crosses between graded warmblood stock and ungraded animals of any breed (i.e. those which have not been accepted into a breeding register of a recognised warmblood breeding society). This complex system will become even more complicated in the future, particularly after 1992 when harmonisation of stud books within the EEC, the lowering of trade barriers, the increasing use of artificial insemination and the development of embryo transplant techniques will change the face of horse breeding.

Today, horses bred in the Hanoverian district are still traditionally given names starting with the first letter of their sires' names. This enables a successful stallion to found his own easily identifiable line, and means that breeders can see at a glance which pedigree and which horse go together. One of the most famous lines, the G-line – which has developed from Goldammer II (born 1919, by Goldschläger I out of an Alderman I mare) and his twenty-seven graded sons, the most important of whom was probably Goldfisch II, who was in turn the grandsire of the outstanding Grande through his son Graf – has been popular since the 1930s and is still extremely successful throughout the world in show jumping and dressage today. When a line, such as the G-line, has proved itself, travellers to almost any horse-breeding country in the world can find animals from that line being used for warmblood breeding. Because of this, the *Verband Hannoverscher Warmblutzüchter*, the Hanoverian Warmblood Breeding Society of West Germany, has a membership that includes many small breeders outside West Germany. The *Verband* therefore sends its representatives from West Germany all over the world to inspect and brand the foals born to Hanoverian registered and graded stock. As would be the case in West Germany, foals to be inspected must have two parents currently graded and registered with the *Verband*, the covering returns of their sires must have been submitted to West Germany for entry into the central computer, and they must be bred and owned by current members of the *Verband* even if the breeders and owners do not live in West Germany. If all these conditions are met then the foal will be issued with Hanoverian pedigree papers by the *Verband* and branded with the H brand on the left thigh. In the 1980s the *Verband* took out copyright on the brand to protect it, and

2

pedigree stallions standing abroad who have completed grading and are registered in West Germany are now also branded with an H on the left side of the neck. (In the mid 1980s a decision was also taken to brand a number on the left side of the neck on Hanoverian foals born in West Germany.)

Over the last fifty years the large numbers of Hanoverian foals bred, and the multiplicity of different crosses available using the established and new bloodlines in the stud books, has meant that a wide range of height, bone and quality has been produced to meet the various demands of the market. From the old-fashioned driving-type horses with straight shoulders, long loins and short croups, through quality, active but powerful show jumpers to the lighter, more elegant horse now finding favour with an increasing number of dressage riders, Hanoverian breeders have tried to fulfil the requirements of equestrian competitors worldwide. This they have done by the judicious crossing of various bloodlines both to strengthen and develop the good points and to minimise the shortcomings which are revealed by the grading process and progeny records. It is this approach, which is designed to bring out in full the particular potential talent inherent in each Hanoverian stallion and mare, that has been the key factor in the successful development of the Hanoverian breed.

In the last twenty years, with the increasing demand for a more athletic competition horse, the modern Hanoverian has changed into a more elegant, quality animal. Breeders are now placing more emphasis on a good shoulder and wither, a more medium-sized height and an improved walk, often through the use of proven crossing between specified lines. This thorough approach now means that everything related to the breeding process is fully documented and the continuing popularity of the Hanoverian breed is based upon its resultant success in fulfilling the modern rider's requirements for a performance horse *par excellence*.

It should be noted that the historical English spelling, Hanoverian, is usually seen in English and American publications in connection with the breed rather than the German double 'n', although the abbreviation 'Hann.' appears in pedigrees and the British Warm-Blood Society has adopted the German spelling.

DEBORAH WALLIN

3

1 Introduction

The Hanoverian is bred on a larger scale than any other German riding horse type. The breeding zone comprises the federal state of Lower Saxony, which includes the cities of Hamburg and Bremen, but does not include the former administrative district of Oldenburg. With around 16,500 registered live broodmares and 290 stallions approved for use in Hanoverian breeding, it is the largest horse-breeding industry in Europe.

The Hanoverian derives its name from the former kingdom of Hanover, which later became the Prussian province of Hanover. It was within these boundaries that

An Artland farm at Grönloh, near Badbergen.

the Hanoverian horse evolved. Appropriately the coat of arms of the present day state of Lower Saxony shows a leaping horse against a red background, which is taken from the shield of the ruling family in Hanover at the time, the Guelphs. The horse had been their emblem since the middle of the fourteenth century.

The crossed horses' heads on the gables of farm houses in Lower Saxony also bear witness to the long-standing association between man and horse.

The Hanoverian is one link in the chain of Western and Central European horse breeds which have developed over the last 300 years in the low-lying coastal areas adjoining the Atlantic, the English Channel, the North Sea and the Baltic, and whose quality has made them famous beyond the boundaries of their country of origin. This chain begins in Brittany (with the Postier Breton) and spreads upwards into northern France (Anglo-Norman, Percheron, Boulonnais), through Belgium (with its Flanders and Brabançon coldbloods) and Holland (Friesian), into Germany (East Friesian, Oldenburg and Hanoverian). The important contribution to this chain from across the Channel (England and Ireland) is the Thoroughbred. From Hanover the chain continues with the Holstein, the Schleswig and Danish coldbloods, the Mecklenburg and Western Pomeranian warmbloods, and finally the Warmblood of Trakehner Origin, which is the last link in the chain.

2 Geography of the Hanoverian breeding zone

Topography

The northern boundary of the breeding zone is the North Sea coast with its three river estuaries of the Elbe, the Weser and the Ems. It is bordered on the north east by the section of the Elbe between Cuxhaven and Schnakenburg, on the east by the German Democratic Republic, and its southern tip contains the town of Münden and is bordered by Hessen. Adjoining its very irregular south-western boundary is the German state of Rhineland-Westphalia, and it is bordered to the west by the Netherlands.

Four-fifths of this zone is made up of flat land. The northern region forms part of the north German coastal plain, bordered by the Mittelland Canal on the south. However, this plain, which covers most of Lower Saxony, is not an unbroken, featureless expanse of land: it consists of various geographical formations and, in parts, some very attractive scenery, even though it lacks high hills or mountains.

The southern triangle, within the area bordered by the towns of Helmstedt, Bückeburg and Münden, is fairly mountainous, containing the Harz mountains and foothills, and including the Süntel, Deister, Ith and Solling hills.

Climate

The north coast has a pronounced maritime climate with prevailing west winds and high rainfall. The climate becomes slightly milder further south. The area as a whole has an average annual rainfall of 695 mm. The southern mountain chains have the highest rainfall (between 800 and 1500 mm), and the eastern districts of Lüchow-Dannenberg and Gifhorn the lowest (560 to 600 mm). It is also worth noting that there are many local variations of climate in the southern valleys. On the coast and in the coastal districts the average variation in temperature between winter and summer is less than in the inland districts. In Nordeney, for example, the variation is on average 15.5 °C, while in Uelzen it is 17.5 °C.

Soil

The zone of salt and freshwater marshland around the North Sea coast and the lower

The Hanoverian breeding zone and stallion stations in 1982.

Hay cart pulled by two Hanoverian mares.

courses of the Elbe, the Weser and the Ems was one of the main birthplaces of the Hanoverian Warmblood. A similar environment exists on the fertile plains alongside the Weser between Bremen and Hanover, alongside its tributaries, the Aller and the Leine, and on the left bank of the Elbe between Hamburg and Schnakenburg. The principal areas of this valuable grazing land lie in the former administrative district of Stade and in East Friesland.

Fine loams ('loess') suitable for cultivation are practically non-existent in the main, northern sector of Lower Saxony. However, they are common in the Schaumburg, Hildesheim, Brunswick and Wolfenbüttel area. Sandy-loam arable land is commonest in the administrative district of Lüneburg and the northern sector of the Hanover administrative district. It is least commonly found in the western part of the former administrative district of Osnabrück. Large zones of diluvial sandy soil are Lüneburg Heath and the spurs which run outwards from it, and Emsland. This sort of soil is almost completely absent in the Hildesheim–Brunswick administrative district. The districts of Stade and Osnabrück contain extensive areas of moorland, most of which has now been 'improved'. These too are almost completely absent in the south.

Lower Saxony is not particularly rich in mineral reserves: there is a little mineral coal (pit coal) near Osnabrück, some lignite (brown coal) near Helmstedt, considerable underground reserves of salt around Lüneburg, Stade and Lüchow, a sizeable amount of potash between Celle and Hildesheim, and also a small quantity of mineral oil, mainly in Emsland. In addition to these, copper, lead, zinc and silver have been mined in the Harz mountains since the Middle Ages.

Agriculture

Lower Saxony is a big cattle-breeding area, and has the highest milk production level of any West German state. It is made up mainly of small farms. A good 75 per cent of the farmland consists of farms of ten to one hundred hectares in size. Large holdings of more than 100 hectares account for only about 5 to 6 per cent of the area.

The north coast area has the largest proportion of grazing land. Many farms in this area have no arable land at all. Inland, the proportion of grazing land is much lower. The southern sector, which accounts for about a fifth of the total area of Lower Saxony, has very little pasture land. Some farms in this area have been completely arable for many years.

There is forestry in the southern mountainous area, on the light, sandy soil of

9

Lüneburg Heath, and in the former administrative district of Osnabrück (Emsland).

Apart from the Volkswagen factory at Wolfsburg, there is no heavy industry. There are various medium-sized industries in the towns of Hanover, Brunswick, Osnabrück, Bremen and Hamburg – the two last-named towns and the rural districts surrounding them also count as part of the Hanoverian breeding area.

3 History of the Hanoverian breeding zone

In the early Middle Ages the area colonised by the Saxons extended from the River Elbe and the River Saale in the east, across present-day Westphalia to the Lower Rhine. After numerous battles, Charlemagne finally incorporated it into his empire. The coast had been colonised by the Frisians. The tribal duchy of the Saxons, in alliance with the Holy Roman Empire, was politically dominant from the tenth to the thirteenth century and produced a significant proportion of the Emperors and German kings. Saxon power reached its peak under the leadership of Henry the Lion from the house of Guelph. He was defeated by the Swabian ruling house of Hohenstaufen. The Guelph territories in the principalities of Lüneburg, Brunswick, Calenberg (Hanover), Northeim and Goslar were reduced, but various branches of the Guelph family ruled in these areas during the following centuries. Since the eleventh century, the Hanse towns of Hamburg and Bremen had been subject directly to the imperial government on account of the importance they had acquired through trade. The archbishopric of Bremen had extended its secular power over most of the so-called 'wet triangle' between the lower courses of the Weser and the Elbe. The Thirty-Years War drew the Guelph territories into a cycle of destruction, heavy taxation and reprisals.

At the end of the seventeenth century the Guelph duchy of Calenberg with its capital, Hanover, through inheritance and conquest had acquired the electorship of the German Empire. In the course of the eighteenth century it also gained the bishoprics of Verden and Osnabrück, the bishopric of Bremen, which had been lost to the Swedes in the Thirty-Years War, and parts of territories around the middle courses of the River Ems.

The choice of the Elector Georg Ludwig of Hanover as King George I of Great Britain brought unity to these two countries through the sovereign. This union lasted until 1837. It led to the electorate of Hanover becoming involved in the rivalries between Britain and France during the Seven-Years War (1756–1763). In the turbulent times of the Napoleonic wars, the former duchy of Hanover was under Prussian rule for three years, and for six years was part of the Kingdom of Westphalia, ruled by King Jerome in Kassel.

The Congress of Vienna (1815) awarded the former Prussian province of East Friesland to Hanover, together with some secularised church possessions. At the same time the electorate became a kingdom, with the sovereign based in London and a viceroy in Hanover. This kingdom was then divided up into administrative districts, which in turn were composed of smaller administrative units.

In 1866, the kingdom was annexed to Prussia, and thus became a Prussian province. This change in political status met with strong protests from a large proportion of the inhabitants, and especially from the rural community. The protests continued well into the twentieth century, though they died down somewhat after the formation of the German *Reich* in 1871.

Hanover remained a province until Prussia was broken up in 1946. It was then combined with the territories of Oldenburg, Brunswick and Schaumburg-Lippe to make the federal state of Lower Saxony. Hanover lost some of its territories when these new divisions were made. The administrative sub-district of Neuhaus, part of the Lüneburg district which lay on the right bank of the Elbe and was famous for its Hanoverian Warmblood breeding, and a few small outposts in the Harz, were incorporated into the Soviet occupation zone, which later became the German Democratic Republic (East Germany).

In the course of various regional reforms, the number of administrative districts and sub-districts was drastically reduced, and the state now comprises the following administrative areas: Lüneburg, Hanover, Brunswick and Oldenburg.

4 Early horse breeding in the Hanover region

The little information we have about the breeding, management and use of horses in this area in the past comes mainly from the flat northern part of Lower Saxony, and makes it clear that horses have been bred in large areas of this region of rich grassland since ancient times.

In the early Middle Ages, horses were often left to breed freely on reserves. Charlemagne left instructions on the management of such reserves. The Saxon leader Henry I, the German king, recruited the war horses he needed for fending off the attacks of the Hungarians from this region. His successor, Henry the Lion, mounted his men on indigenous horses for his campaigns east of the Elbe.

The coats of arms of old farming families from the Lower Weser area contain half an imperial eagle. This honour is said to have been granted to members of these families for their part in the Italian campaigns of Frederick Barbarossa, leader of Swabia and a member of the house of Hohenstaufen. During the fifteenth and sixteenth centuries the dukes of Hoya, whose territory later passed through inheritance into the hands of the Guelph family, had a stud in Bücken, near Hoya on the Weser. The horses bred there were mostly sired by Spanish stallions and had a good reputation throughout the country. The stud was later merged with the *Hofgestüt* Memsen, discussed below.

During the Thirty-Years War, George, Duke of Brunswick–Lüneburg set up the 'Lüneburg Corps', containing three cavalry regiments mounted on homebred horses, and placed it at the disposal of the Swedish king, Gustavus Adolphus. His successors later supported the Emperor and other warring princes by supplying them with mounted troops. The governor of the Netherlands, which was under Spanish occupation at the time, spoke very highly of such troops in about 1675, saying he had never seen a better cavalry than the Hanoverian. In 1693 the English cavalry obtained part of its supply of remounts from Hanover. Around 1700 the famous dragoons of the Swedish King Karl XII, who was fighting campaigns throughout Europe, were mounted on horses bred in what were then the Swedish duchies of Bremen and Verden.

Since even in those days there were few large estates or agricultural holdings in Hanover (unlike Holstein and Mecklenburg), it was the Guelph dukes who set the pace with their court studs located about the country. Local farmers also benefited from the services of the stallions kept at these studs. There were court studs at

13

Memsen, near Hoya (as already mentioned), at Radbruch (near Lüneburg), and at Nienover and Neuhas (both in the Solling hills).

From the above it is clear that for centuries the larger horse-breeding areas have been producing not only horses suitable for work on the land, but highly bred horses whose courage, size and agility made them suitable for use as riding horses (i.e. as cavalry horses).

By now, the heavy horses used by the knights in hand-to-hand combat had become redundant with the introduction of firearms many years earlier. The court studs, the few large landowners who existed in the area between the Elbe, the Harz mountains and the Weser, and their counterparts in other regions of Germany were all trying to breed horses which fitted in with the new image. They were up-grading the rather coarse, placid indigenous animal through the use of stallions from Spain and southern Italy in order to produce a more highly bred horse with better carriage, a more expressive head and more showy paces; in short they wanted a spirited horse which caught the eye and carried itself proudly. The Spanish and Italian stallions, which contained large doses of Arab, Barb and other Oriental blood, had already begun to appear in the court studs at the beginning of the sixteenth century. They came either as the spoils of war, as presents to the prince, or from dealers. In time their influence spread to the flat-land studs. The farmers found it profitable to sell the resulting 'improved' youngstock back to the prince or duke, whose studs often failed to supply sufficient numbers of animals for his use, or to sell them off as cavalry remounts. In fact it is fair to say that at least that part of the future kingdom of Hanover which had the best grazing, soil and climatic conditions had a flourishing horse-breeding industry and an important export market long before the days of state aid and intervention.

5 The creation of the Hanoverian breed and its development

1735–1850

The Electorate of Hanover had had personal links with the kingdom of Britain since 1714. Absolutism, which had grown up in France under Louis XIII and Louis XIV, was followed by the spread of mercantilism in Europe. The ruler found himself being forced to increase receipts so that he could cover the cost of maintaining the army and the administrative apparatus. In order to obtain a favourable balance of trade, the national agricultural and industrial output had to be increased, so as to encourage more exports. At the same time, imports had to be kept within limits.

George II, Elector of Hanover, took a historic step in the history of Hanoverian horse breeding in 1735 when he decreed:

> therefore for the benefit of our subjects and in order to promote horse breeding in our German lands, especially in the duchy of Bremen and the county of Hoya . . . we shall set up a public stud [*Landgestüt*], as a special favour, with twelve stallions to start with, and this stud shall exist for the present and until such time as it has been seen what good comes of it for the land as a whole.

One of the aims of setting up this stud, which was financed from the sovereign's private funds for the first few decades of its existence, was to improve the quality of the many farm-bred horses, most of which were sired by inferior stallions since there was no compulsory stallion licensing. By improving the quality, the horses would be made more attractive to military buyers, who at the time bought all their remounts in Holstein and Mecklenburg where horses were an important export commodity.

Roger Brown, presumably an Englishman, who was at the time first huntsman of the staghounds based at Celle, was commissioned to go to Holstein to buy the twelve stallions. Over the preceding decades a breed of horse known as the 'Holstein Black' had evolved on the large estates of that region, and had gained a reputation all over Europe as an ideal riding and cavalry horse. The famous horseman de la Guérinière said of them in 1730 that they were well made and had beautiful paces, and that they made outstanding high school horses and splendid carriage horses.

In the spring of 1736 the new Celle stud set up its 'covering places' (stallion stations) for the first time on the marshes of the Lower Elbe between Stade and

Neuhaus (Oste), and near the middle reaches of the Weser between Stolzenau and Hoya. We know the names of some of the stallions:

The fine black Gyldenstein,
The big golden bay Gyldenstein,
The fine black Reventlow,
The small black Ranzau,
The medium-sized black Hammerstein,
The big, black rough-coated Ahlefeld.

As well as telling us that the predominant colour was black, these descriptions also show the estate of origin of each horse, since the names are those of large Holstein landowners. The following interesting and rather quaint set of instructions was issued to the 'stallion men':

1. The stud fee is one himbten [an old German measure of approximately 20 kg or 40 lb] of oats.
2. The additional sum of one thaler is due on the birth of a live foal.
3. Precise instructions for the management, care and handling of the stallions are to be adhered to.
4. Notification of arrival to be given to the relevant authorities, together with reports on the stallions and stud business. Reports to be monthly.
5. Only forty to fifty mares to be covered by each stallion. Each stallion may serve two to three times per day.
6. Small or ugly mares not expected to produce a good foal may only be covered with the permission of the breeding authorities.
7, Mares which do not hold to the service are to be sent home. Any one mare may only be covered three to four times, or at the most five times, in one stud season.
8. Farmers' mares are to be given priority over the mares of noblemen and officers.
9. Stallion returns, foal lists and feed lists are to be kept and certified by the authorities in accordance with instructions.
10. Behaviour: no smoking, no imbibing at the hostelries, coverings and stud business to be supervised personally.

These instructions have been modified in the 250-odd years since the stud was founded, but the principles remain the same.

At first the stallions from the royal stud were received with mistrust by the local farmers. However, this mistrust gradually subsided and the number of visiting mares increased, as did the number of stallions. In 1745 there were fifty stallions at stud, and about 2000 mares were covered. The Seven-Years War brought setbacks and many horses were lost. Up until 1770, replacements came mainly from Holstein, though individual stallions from England, Spain, southern Italy and Trakehnen were already being used. Furthermore, the court studs at Neuhaus (Solling) and Memsen (Hoya) received instructions to make their stallions available for the use of the farmers. In 1776, the Celle stud, which had up until that point been maintained by the ruler personally, became the responsibility of the government authorities.

From 1770 onwards, replacement stallions were not bought in Holstein but in Mecklenburg, and sometimes in England. The Mecklenburg had a similar reputation in Europe to that which the Holstein had enjoyed fifty years previously. About forty years after the establishment of the public stud, there were between fifty and sixty stallions at Celle, and during the stud season these stallions stood in the marshes and lowlands of the rivers: on the Elbe between Bleckede and Cuxhaven, on the Weser between Stolzenau and Stotel, on the Aller and Leine between Coldingen and Ilten above Hanover, and at Celle itself and Verden. The upland areas and moors away from the rivers were mainly served by private stallions. By 1800, the number of state stallions for public use had risen to 100. From the year the stud was founded to the turn of the century, 242,774 mares were taken to state stallions. In the last decades of the eighteenth century, 10,000 foals and remounts per year were sold for export at an annual sum of 400,000 thalers. Admittedly the majority were sired by privately owned stallions, but the quality of the latter had also improved as an indirect effect of the state stud.

A large proportion of the horses ridden and driven by Hanoverian troops were now homebred, which meant that one of the aims of the stud had been fulfilled in a relatively short time. However, the Napoleonic wars were to destroy all that had been achieved. Between 1803 and 1815 the activities of the stud were severely curtailed because the stallions had to be rescued from the hands of the French troops.

In the new Kingdom of Hanover which emerged after the Congress of Vienna, the reconstruction of the horse-breeding industry was tackled with single-minded determination. Efforts were made to increase the stock of stallions at Celle. The private stocks of mares had been decimated by the campaigns, and these were built up again by making good mares from the disbanded dragoon regiments available to the

Da sich der Ruf von der Brauchbarkeit, Schönheit und Dauerhaftigkeit der mehresten - vermittelst des Land - Gestüdts in hiesigen Landen erzielten Füllens, wie Uns glaubhaft versichert worden, nunmehro nach Wunsch auswärtiger Orten solchergestalt verbreitet, daß man Ursache hat, diese Art Füllen zum Besten ihrer Verkäufer mit eigentlichen bewährten Kennzeichen zu versehen, gestalt dann verschiedene Districte sich bereits ausgebeten, das gewöhnliche Brennen einzuführen, um fremden Käufern dadurch eine hinlängliche Versicherung in Rücksicht auf die Gestüdt- mäßige Raçe darstellen zu können; So benachrichtigen Wir Euch hiedurch, wasmaaßen gut gefunden worden, denen - zu allen Bedeckungs - Oertern abgehenden Land- Gestüdt - Knechten erforderliche Brenn - Eisen, welche das Zeichen

enthalten, unter der Anweisung mitzugeben, wie sie die Land - Gestüdt - Füllen auf der linken Lende ohnentgeldlich behutsam brennen sollen.

Es muß zwar solches an Seiten der Eigenthümer ohne allen Zwang verstattet werden, indessen nehmen Wir die Sache doch für ein sicheres Beförderungs - Mittel, den Land - Gestüdt - Füllen - Handel, immer noch mehr in Aufnahme zu bringen, und hegen dahero zu Euch das Vertrauen, Ihr werdet nicht unterlassen, denen - den Nutzen von obiger Veranstaltung mißkennenden Unterthanen, das diensame Brennen der Füllens bestens anzupreisen.

Wir *sind euch zu gnädig. Willfahrung ge-*

neigt

Hannover, den 3ten Febr. 1768.

Königl. Großbritannische, zur Churf. Braunsch. Lüneb.
Cammer, verordnete Cammer - Præsident, Geheime - Rähte,
Geheime - Cammer - auch Cammer - Rähte.

G. A. v. Münchhausen.

Meinersen

farmers. The farmers paid half of the price, and the government (the *Domänenkammer*) paid the rest. In exchange, the farmers had to give an undertaking that the mare would be covered for four years by a state stallion and that the first filly foal would be kept, and would be used for three years as a brood mare.

In 1823, the army remount committee began buying direct from the breeders as well as from dealers. Up until that point it had obtained its supplies almost exclusively from dealers. By 1818 the number of state stallions had risen again to 100 (in 1815 there had been only forty-seven). The purpose of the state stallions, which continued to be stationed in the marshy districts, was mainly to produce well-bred horses for riding and military use. In addition to these stallions, fifty to sixty horses from the royal stables also stood at stud every year in the administrative districts (*Landdrosteien*) of Lüneburg and Hanover. The large numbers of farm horses which were needed were mostly sired by privately owned stallions, which outnumbered the state stallions by at least three to one.

In the administrative district of Stade privately owned stallions already required approval before they were allowed to stand at stud. They had to be examined by a committee of experts, which had been specially set up for the purpose, who assessed their value for breeding. In 1844 a Licensing Order, applying to the whole of the kingdom, was passed and put into practice. East Friesland, which had recently become part of the kingdom of Hanover, had been covered by such an order since 1715.

The high standard of Hanoverian horse breeding is borne out by the following description which was given by a foreign expert:

> If you should wish to see what advantages are to be derived from a public stud [*Landgestüt*], you should visit the region of Hanover, where the well-being of the farmers is largely due to the public stud, and where the broodmares owned by the farmers are often better than those to be found in the stables of princes.

During this period, the first half of the nineteenth century, the foundations were laid with this public stud for the development of the modern Hanoverian Warmblood.

(Opposite page)
Branding order from 1768 for foals sired by stallions from the Celle stud. The order explains that branding has become necessary to give the buyer a guarantee that he has bought a genuine product, since horses bred in Hanover are highly sought after. It adds that branding will also serve to spread the breed's fame even further.

An important part was played by two directors of this stud: the brothers August von Spörcken (director 1816–1839) and Friedrich von Spörcken (1839–1866).

As we have seen, in the first decades of the stud's existence the founders of the Hanoverian breed were mostly stallions containing Spanish and Italian blood bought in Holstein and Denmark, but from about 1775 homebred stallions from Mecklenburg and England began to dominate the scene. Mecklenburg and its neighbour, Western Pomerania, had a high proportion of large estates and farms, and on these they developed in the eighteenth century a high-class horse, based on Oriental foundations, which enjoyed a good reputation among the horsemen of Europe. Just before the turn of the century, enterprising breeders had already begun importing English Thoroughbreds bred for the racecourse. These were used in Mecklenburg either for Thoroughbred breeding or for crossing with Mecklenburg mares (the latter with very good results).

The Celle state stud and the court studs at Memsen and Neuhaus had already bought some of these Mecklenburgs and English Thoroughbreds before the turn of the century. After 1815, Mecklenburg became the main source of stallions for the Celle stud. A large proportion of Mecklenburg was owned by a small number of families, who had developed studs whose names were famous. Among these were the studs of the Counts of Plessen at Ivenack, the Freiherren von Biel at Zierow and Weitendorf, the Michael family at Ihlenfeld, and the Counts Hahn at Basedow. They had achieved their success through importing the right animals from England and through 'feeling their way'. They were also aided by the favourable conditions for rearing horses which existed in the area. These studs bred Thoroughbreds and warmbloods derived from crossing Thoroughbred stallions with 'improved' Mecklenburg mares.

In Hanoverian pedigrees, a Thoroughbred is denoted by XX after its name, and the following Thoroughbred stallions gained a particularly good reputation: Robin Hood XX (1818) by Muley, who was imported from England and stood at Zierow; Morwick Ball XX and his son Herodot XX (Ivenack); Grosvenor XX (Ihlenfeld); and Wildfire XX by Waxy (Redefin Central Stud). In 1838, 80 per cent of the Hanoverian state stallions were from Mecklenburg. At first, Hanover acquired its English Thoroughbred stallions from Mecklenburg, but from 1830 onwards it also imported them directly from England.

Around 1840 a landmark had been reached in the state stud's history which is also to be seen as a turning point in the history of Hanoverian Warmblood breeding: some of the stallions were still provided by the royal stables in Hanover, but at least one-third of the total stallion population was now Thoroughbred, and the remaining two-thirds were either halfbred or quarterbred.

1850–1920

From 1844 onwards, stallions standing in any region of Hanover had to be licensed. Because of the higher standards which now had to be reached, the number of privately owned stallions fell. State stallion stations began to gain a foothold in the upland areas. However, more intensive farming and the increase in the amount of heavy root crops grown meant that a heavier horse was now required. Mecklenburg could no longer help; in fact, its own studs were facing the same problems.

The brothers August and Friedrich von Spörcken had good connections in both Mecklenburg and England. They had gained international recognition for their knowledge and skill. The fifty-year period during which they gave their services to the horse-breeding industry in Hanover is considered the foundation period for the development of the modern Hanoverian.

During his many visits to England for the purpose of buying horses, Friedrich von Spörcken had become acquainted with that excellent form of transport, the mail coach. In particular he had noticed the horses, which were mostly large-framed, with substance, and possessed of great courage and endurance. They were capable of galloping for long periods without showing any great signs of tiredness. They had mostly been developed by using Thoroughbred blood on native foundation mares, especially those originating from the counties of Yorkshire and Norfolk, and from the Holderness area of East Yorkshire.

Between 1830 and 1890 about 100 stallions of the English coach type were used at the state stud. Their large frames and their substance made them very popular with breeders, and they played a part in the development of the modern Hanoverian. The most famous of these stallions were as follows:

NABOCKLISH by Y Spencer (chestnut), born 1854 in England, founder of a strong Hanoverian line (Schlütter).
SEBRAS (grey), born 1840 in England, state stallion at Celle 1846–63.
HOLDERNESS (grey), born 1838 in England, state stallion at Celle 1844–61.
CHAMPION by Coachman, (bay), born 1849 in England, state stallion at Celle 1852–77; in his twenty-six years at stud he covered 1945 mares and achieved a high success rate.

Sebras, an English part-Thoroughbred, state stallion at Celle from 1846 to 1863.

(Opposite page)
Holderness, Yorkshire Coach Horse, state stallion at Celle 1844–1861.
Champion by Coachman, Yorkshire Coach Horse, state stallion at Celle 1852–1877.

Interestingly enough, Sebras and Holderness were bought in spite of having unknown pedigrees.

However, the main role in the creation of a native Hanoverian horse breed was played by the following stallions, and it is they who are the real foundation stallions of the Hanoverian breed: two Pomeranian-bred horses, the black Zernebog by Jupiter (1845), who was at Celle from 1849 to 1871, and the bay Jellachich by Defensive XX, who was born in 1844 at the famous Brook stud in Western Pomerania, and served as a state stallion from 1850 to 1866; and thirdly the bay Norfolk, by Y Seymour, who was born in 1843 in Mecklenburg, and was based at Celle from 1849 to 1871. These stallions stood mainly at the Oterson stallion station in the Aller marshes near Verden, making their influence felt in the main breeding zones of the time: the districts of Lüneburg, Land Hadeln and Kehdingen.

Individual stallions bred in Hanover had been in use at the Celle stud before 1860, but after this date the number of homebred stallions rose sharply, and by the end of the century they accounted for about 90 per cent of the total stallion population. One of the most outstanding examples of a Hanoverian-bred stallion was Flick, by Zernebog out of Cita by Jellachich, who was born in 1860 at the Herrenhausen stud. This stallion stood at stud in the Elbe marshes near Lüneburg for twenty-four years, transmitting his highly acclaimed qualities of substance, powerful build, breeding, and excellent paces to almost 800 foals.

The Herrenhausen court stud deserves a mention here for the impetus it gave to Hanoverian horse breeding. It was founded in 1844 and situated in the lime-rich Leine marshes west of Hanover. Its main purpose up until 1866 was to supply horses for the royal stables. This stud was also the last place where the famous Hanoverian Creams, the ceremonial coach horses of the Hanoverian monarchs, were bred. [These creams (in fact cremellos) were of necessity very inbred and their consequent tendencies to being short-lived and needing false tails for parade purposes caused them to die out before the end of the nineteenth century; pub. note.] Outstanding environmental conditions and expert management enabled Herrenhausen to contribute a disproportionately large number of high-class stallions to the Hanoverian breeding industry in the eighty-five years of its existence. It survived until 1929.

(Opposite page)
Pedigrees of Zernebog, Jellachich and Norfolk. The symbols show repeated sire lines, and family numbers are given. 'Stute von' = mare by. 'Y' and 'O' stand for 'Young' and 'Old', although Eclipse, great great grandson of the Darley Arabian, normally takes no prefix.

Left table

H. 1849—71. —			
Zernebog (R. H. — 1845)			
Antigone		angebl. XX Jupiter	
Miß Gigg	Blak Comet 3	Miß. unb.	Protector 2
	Cinderella 3 / Robin Hood 1		Comus 25 / Emma 2
St. von St. v. Y. Wh. / Granicus 12 / St. von Y. Wh. / Miß Witch 1 / Shuffler 4 / Sorcerer 6 ▼ Y. G. / Whaley 6 / Eleanor 6 Y. G. / Sorcerer 6 ▼ Y. G.			Houghton Laß 25 / Don Calsaß 6 / Belta 2 / Sorcerer 6 ● ▼ Y. G. Giantes ▼

Right table

H. 1850—1866. — gez. i. Pommern. —			
Jellachich (br. H. — 1844)			
Beauty (Jrl.)		2 Defensive	
		Stute von 2	Defence 5
		Stute von 2 / Selim 2	Defiance 5 / Whale= bone 1
Fair Ellen 2		Buzzard 3 / Alexander=Stute / Witchcraft 9 / Little Folly 5 / Rubens 2 ● Aleg.=St. 2	Warn 18 / Penelope 1

Pedigree

```
                              ┌ Delpini ─────── ┌ Highflyer   -Herod
                  ┌ Seymour ──┤                 └ Counteß     -Blank
                  │           └ BayJavelin ───── ┌ Javelin    -O Eclipse
       ┌ YSeymour ┤                              └ YFlora     -Highflyer
       │          │             ┌ YDickAndrews ─ ┌ DickAndrews  JoeAndrews-O Eclipse
       │          └ Tamborina ──┤                └ MissWatt     Delpini
Norfolk┤                        └ Hambletonian ─ ┌ Hambletonian KingFergus - O Eclipse
       │                                         └ Stute von    D Drone
       │             ┌ Napoleon ─┌ Cardinal ──── ┌ GuyMannering ┌ Chanticleer
       └ Stute von ──┤           │               │      X X     │   v. Woodpecker
                     │           └ Medusa        │              │   v. O Eclipse
                     └ mecklenburgische Stute ─── └ englischeSt. └ Stute v. D Drone

              I         II        III        IV        V   VI   VII

Drone:   VI  V
Eclipse: VII  V,VI,VI.
```

Norfolk by Y. Seymour, at Celle 1849–1871.

(Opposite page)
Zernebog by Jupiter, at Celle 1849–1871.
Jellachich by Defensive, at Celle 1850–1866.

Herrenhausen Park, around 1830.

Hanover set about becoming a top breeding area of powerful, forward-going warmbloods. The structure of its agriculture meant that there was from the outset a shortage of large areas of good quality pasture suitable for rearing young horses. Hanoverian breeders were mostly small farmers with insufficient land for rearing horses up to the age of three or four. This meant that they tended to sell the horses as foals. The Hanoverian government and the state stud had been trying since 1815 to persuade larger landowners and tenants to take on young stallions for rearing, but never with much success. Hence from the middle of the century onwards increasing numbers of Hanoverian-bred foals were sold to Mecklenburg, Pomerania and to a lesser extent Brandenburg, to be reared by large landowners who were in a position to provide larger areas of better grazing. Over the decades, Mecklenburg became the largest outlet for Hanoverian youngstock, which were then either bought back by the Celle stud as stallion material or sold as military remounts or farm horses.

By offering breeders stallions with substance and good breeding, the Hanoverian stud administration managed to halt the advance of the coldblood type of horse. The experience of Mecklenburg, Western Pomerania and Brandenburg had served as a warning in this respect.

It is understandable that the state administration both in Hanoverian and Prussian times should turn its thoughts to the question of army remounts. In contrast to many other breeding areas, however, a compromise was achieved. In the second half of the nineteenth century, as a result of negotiations between the stud authorities and agents representing the interests of the farmers, it was agreed that a type of horse would be bred which met the requirements of the army as regards toughness, endurance and courage, while still providing the substance, even temperament and fertility required by the farmers.

Farm horse stallions had been mostly privately owned, but after 1850 public stallion stations spread to the upland areas, and the situation began to change. State stallions, whose main task had been to produce army remounts and quality riding and carriage horses, also assumed the responsibility for providing horses for agriculture. In 1867 a breeding policy was formulated for the first time by the *Verein zur Förderungde Hannoverschen Landespferdezucht* (Society for the Promotion of Hanoverian Horse Breeding). The aim was 'To produce a large, powerful horse with substance, a strong coach horse and at the same time a useful army horse.'

The breed began to become established after 1850 with the help of English coach horse and trotting breeds, and above all through the foundation stallions Zernebog, Jellachich, Norfolk and Flick. The last two, especially Norfolk, transmitted to their stock exactly what was wanted (i.e. height, a large frame, substance, soundness and fertility). Many of their progeny were used at stud, and they left their stamp on the Hanoverian for generations. It was the first time in the breed's history that it had been 'stamped' to this degree.

Coronation coach of King George I, drawn by Hanoverian Creams, from a painting at Herrenhausen.

Cream Herrenhausen Hanoverian from a painting in Cumberland House, Gmunden, Austria.

Although in time other lines were established, at the turn of the century very many Hanoverians in use as breeding stock were inbred to Norfolk and Flick. Norfolk appears four times and Flick and Zernebog twice in the pedigree of Schwabenstreich, who produced fifty-three stallions for use in the Hanoverian breeding programme.

As we have said, the horses were bred in Hanover and then sent to Mecklenburg to be reared. This system was found to work well. There was a good market for Hanoverian breeding stock, especially stallions, in the northern German breeding areas such as Oldenburg, Holstein, Mecklenburg, Pomerania and Brandenburg.

The emphasis on breeding stock descended from Norfolk and Flick ceased at the beginning of the twentieth century when the breed authorities realised that there was a risk of the horses becoming too big and at the same time losing some of their courage and action. New bloodlines superceded those of the foundation stock. The most important of these were the progeny of the English-bred Thoroughbreds Kingdom XX (at Celle 1882–1898) and Devils Own XX (1894–1906), and of Adeptus XX (1884–1904), who was bred at Herrenhausen and was also a

1902—	Schwabenstreich (R. H. — 1897)	Schwabe	Schlucker	Schlütter	Nabocklish
					Dechant-Stute
				Stute von	Bravo II
					St. von — St. v. + Norfolk
			Stute von	Flor	⊙ Flick
					St. von — Norkit + Norfolk
				Stute von	Nordlicht St. von ‡ Norfolk / Y. C. XX
					Alhambra-Stute
		Stute von	Leo	Leonidas II	+ Norfolk
					⊙ Zernebog-Stute
				Stute von	Harry
					St. von — Reinecke d. J. ■ Y. C. XX
			Stute von	Voltigeur	■ Y. Confederate
					Tancred II-Stute
				Stute von	Jupiter — Y. Premier
					—

Pedigree of Schwabenstreich, black horse foaled 1897, showing repeated lines to Norfolk, Flick–Zernebog, and Y. Confederate.

Schwabenstreich by Schwabe, state stallion at Celle 1902–1922.

Thoroughbred. Another stallion used was Nelusko by the East Prussian Neckar, out of a grand-daughter of Flick. He stood at stud from 1900 to 1925. It was these stallions and their progeny who ensured that the Hanoverian produced in the top breeding zones remained a highly bred, well-muscled animal with a good saddle position, harmonious outlines and elastic paces.

The male lines of Devils Own and Adeptus still survive 100 years later. The male line of Flick can also still be found in the pedigrees of modern stallions.

It was in the last quarter of the nineteenth century that the horses from the different Hanoverian breeding zones developed their individual characteristics, which reflected the agricultural structure, the amount of grazing available to the breeder, and the quality of the state stallions available in the zone. These characteristics remained up until about 1960, which marked the beginning of the modern era, that of the pure riding horse.

The Lower Elbe region, containing the areas of Altes Land, Kehdingen and Land Hadeln, and the best-known stallion stations (Jork, Drochtersen, Baljerdorf, Kehdingbruch and Altenbruch), produced large-framed horses which had substance but were often lacking in 'breeding'. The Wursten area between Cuxhaven and Bremerhaven produced the heaviest type of horse and the coarsest. The Elbe marshes in the Lüneburg region, with the stallion stations of Brietlingen, Handorf and Hohnstorf, had finer, more highly bred mares. The horses bred in the Weser and Aller marshes in the Hoya and Verden districts were of similar type. This area contained the stallion stations of Otersen, Stedebergen, Hoyahagen and Thedinghausen, which stood many highly bred stallions, and is the home of the Hanoverian Halfbred racehorse. The youngest of the top breeding zones grew up around the Badbergen stallion station in Artland, north of Osnabrück. This zone, with its medium textured upland soil, produced a practical horse with harmonious outlines, primarily suited to work on the land.

The decades leading up to the First World War were influenced by the work of Dr Grabensee, who was *Landstallmeister* at Celle from 1892 to 1915 and who left his mark on the development and reputation of the Hanoverian. The *Hannoversche Stutbuchgesellschaft* (Hanoverian Breed Society) had been established in 1888, with

(Opposite page)
Kingdom XX, state stallion at Celle 1882–1898.
Adeptus XX by Adonis, state stallion at Celle 1884–1904.

the aim of drawing up a breed register. In 1900, the President, General von Troschke, defined the aim of the breeding policy as follows:

> A horse suitable for use as a troop horse, heavy cavalry horse, artillery horse or middle-weight carriage horse, having a good, regular, ground-covering action in both trot and canter. It must have a good temperament and be able to take things in its stride. The use of 'blood' must be coupled with good sense. Horses which do not meet these conditions must be suitable for use as farm horses and must be able to plough a furrow thirty centimetres wide.
>
> The horse must have a pleasing outline, a well set on neck and tail, a sloping shoulder, correct limbs with well-defined joints and tendons, and good feet with well-developed frogs.
>
> In walk and trot the horse must move straight. Horses which are broad across the hips are frowned upon, since it is difficult to keep condition on them.

It seems from this description that army horses were given preference in the breeding programme, though it must be taken into account that artillery horses were little more than farm horses. The proportion of English Thoroughbred stallions at the state stud at this time was about 3 per cent.

To counteract the in-breeding to Norfolk and the other foundation stallions, Grabensee introduced more East Prussians, including some from the central studs of Graditz and Beberbeck. Colorado, Comet and Opticus (all by Optimus), Orinocco (by Perkunos) and Lorbeer (by Whitebait XX) all came from the Beberbeck central stud. Anselm by Primogenitus, Morgenstern by Morgengruss, Sport by General XX, Gessler by Fantast, Erlkönig by Erdgeist and Sileen by Bülow came from East Prussian private breeders. Standing, as they did, at stallion stations which had been in existence for a long time, they tended to cover mares from established bloodlines and were therefore able to make their influence felt to a high degree. Another outside stallion introduced was the grey purebred Arabian Amurath I by Amurath OX [OX denotes an Arab; pub. note], born at the Austrian state stud of Radautz in 1897. In fourteen seasons at stud this horse sired eleven Hanoverian stallions and had a positive influence on paces as well as an upgrading effect on the Hanoverian breed. However, the sire lines founded by all the above stallions disappeared after varying lengths of time.

An example of the pedigree of a Hanoverian horse bred in the Land Hadeln breeding zone during this period is shown opposite. Nerodella was a three-year-old filly who won a 'la-Preis' in her class (light riding and driving horse type) at the DLG

Flendra								Nelusko							
Stute von				Flenheim				Finette				Neckar			
Stute von		Albany 23		Blüthe		● Flick		Stute von		Fiesco II		Naemi		Percival	
Stute	Güstrow	Bariolette 23	Salvator 13	Stute von	Blenheim 1	Cita	Zernebog	Stute von	🔲 Augur	Stute von	● Flick	🔲 Nanny	Atleth	Peranga	Lahire 43
Nord v. X Norfolk / St. v. Y. Haronindes	Y. Protector v. Protector 2 / Mierendorfer Stute	Orphelia 1 / Babette 23	Dollar 1 / Sauvagine 13	⌐St. v. X Norfolk / Schlütter	Chevalier d'Industrie 2 / Tyburnia 1	Jellachich / Favanella	Jupiter × × v. Protector 2 / Antigone	Römer {Tüchtig — X Norfolk / St. v. Honnenhengst ⌐Schlütter	Belfort 8 / Anna	Martaban / St. v. Fingal II	Stute v. Jellachich / Zernebog	Belfort 8 / Nettina	Weissenburg (3/4) X Norfolk / Stute v. Athleth v. {St. v. Jella. / Zernebog / ▲Sahama 3	Oromedon / Portia	▲Sahama 3 / Luna 43

Pedigree of Nerodella, dark brown mare foaled 1907.

(German agricultural society) show in Hamburg in 1910. The stallions Neckar and Augur were both East Prussian. Flick appears twice and Norfolk four times. The first Thoroughbred, Albany, is in the third generation.

In the period from 1907 to 1918 the demand for remounts increased on account of the growth of the army and the heavy losses incurred during the First World War. The above-mentioned warmbloods imported from foreign studs played a major part in meeting this demand.

1920–1982

The First World War caused heavy losses – even broodmares were requisitioned – but the actual foundations remained. The devaluation of currency in the postwar years led to a rush to invest in things which would hold their value. Consequently equine breeding stocks rose sharply.

In 1922 the *Verband Hannoverscher Warmblutzüchter* (Hanoverian Warmblood Society) was formed. It took over the responsibilities of the *Stutbuchgesellschaft* and served the interests of breeders in all matters, with particular emphasis on the agricultural aspects. In 1925 another state stud was established, at Osnabrück-Eversburg, to cope with the increased numbers of state stallions – by now nearly 600.

A cause of major cut-backs in the Hanoverian breeding industry, as in all the other German warmblood breeding industries, was the sharp drop in the number of remounts required by the military authorities. Every year 2500 horses bred in the Hanover region and reared either there or in the territories east of the Elbe had been sold through this outlet. After 1918, this number dropped by more than half.

In the period between the two world wars, the Hanoverians bred in the main breeding zones increased in bone and substance to the point where they were hardly recognisable as light (as opposed to agricultural) warmbloods any longer. The reasons for this were not hard to discover. In a word, the market – the customers, that is – demanded a heavier horse. There was not much of a market for remounts, and in these difficult times there was little demand for sport horses. Substance and bone, gauged by the measurement around the cannon bone below the knee, became an essential factor in assessing the merit and value of a horse for the purpose of buying foals or breeding stock, for awarding prizes, or for licensing stallions. Even the army paid more for a coarse artillery horse with a lot of bone than for a potential cavalry horse.

Among the most sought-after stallions of this period were the state stallion Schwabenstreich and those of his progeny whose pedigree traced back to the Schlucker–Schlütter–Nabocklish line. Many representatives of this line displayed great courage and action combined with compact 'cobbiness' and substance. A good example is the stallion Schorse II by Schwof I, who was a state stallion at Celle from 1927 to 1940. Another example of the heavier type is the state stallion Journalist by Jasperding, who came from the Jason line and stood at stud from 1927 to 1945. Nineteen of his sons stood at stud in Hanover.

The male line of Adeptus XX was very widespread during this period. Alnok, his son Alderman I and their descendants had taken the place of the Norfolk line, and also of the line of Nelusko. Horses from this 'A-line' were already characterised in this period by size and a large frame, and were often powerful, large-boned types, predominantly chestnut in colour with a lot of white markings. Alderman I (1909)

Schorse II by Schwof I, state stallion at Celle 1927–1940.

Journalist by Jasperding, state stallion at Celle 1927–1945.

Pedigree of **Journalist** (left) — header: geb. 1925 F. 179/169 200 22.4

Journalist							
Abotina				Jasperding			
		Altist		Nannecke		Jasmund	
Machteld	Neding		Alnok	Dolinde	Naber	Normannia	Jasal

Lower generations (read by column, left → right):

g5	Flustra / Macdonald • Nelusko • Julius • Adeptus xx • *Derb • Piccina / Nadick • Nordend • Jason
g6	Macdonald • Monarch xx • *Derb St. v. ●Fl. • Flenheim ●Fl. • St. v. Fiesco II ●Fl. • Y. Baptist xx • St. v. ●Fl. • St. v. ●Fl. • ■Nord /Nf. u. ○E. • Nording ■Nord / u. ○ • St. v. ●Fl. • Piccolomini xx • Nadock /Nf. • Corrector • ■Nord /Nf. u. ○E. • Salow xx

Pedigree of **Schorse I u. II** (right) — header:
I. geb. 1920 F. 176/166 192 21.0
II. geb. 1923 F. 174/164 203 22.6

Schorse I u. ll							
Nubandina				Schwof I			
Almweide		Nordland		Orena		Schwaben-streich	
Anigia	Alcalde		Nobleman	Magnhild	Oheim		Schwabe

Lower generations (read by column, left → right):

g5	Schwätzerin • Anselm • Ahorn • Landstreicher xx • Nordlicht • Maas • Die Flatterhafte Flenheim • Optimist • Leo • ●Schlucker
g6	●Schlucker / Schl. • Schwätzerin • Anselm • Ketzer • Landstreicher xx • Miller Nord ■ u. △E. • Nordlicht • Ulrich • Norfolk • ■Nordfolk • Julius /Schl. u. ▲Fl.-St. • Maas • Die Flatterhafte Flenheim ▲Fl. • Optimist • Leo • Flor ▲Fl. • Leonidas II ■Nf. • Voltigeur • ●Schlüter / Schl.

Pedigrees of Journalist and Schorse I and II. Figures at the top of the pedigree show their height, girth and bone (in cm).

stood at stud from 1912 to 1932 in Drochtersen, and had an enormous influence on Hanoverian breeding via his progeny, seventy-one of which became state stallions and 206 of which were registered mares.

In 1938 there were eighty state stallions belonging to this line, i.e. 22.2 per cent of the total. However, the strongest bloodline, which in this same year had 111 representatives (30.8 per cent of the total), was the Fling–Flingarth–Flenheim–Flick line. The two outstanding stallions from this line in the period between the wars were Feiner Kerl and Flavius, both by Fling.

Alnok by Adeptus XX, state stallion at Celle 1896–1913.

Feiner Kerl by Fling, state stallion at Celle 1922–1943.

Fling / Rebanja								
Fling dbr.	**Flingarth** br. / dbr.	Flenheim dbr.	☦ Flick dbr.	Zernebog				
			Blüthe	Blenheim xx	●	▲		
		Kimbale	∎ King br.	Kingdom xx	▲	↑		
			Hospodella	Hospodar	●↾			
	Kilbe br.	∎ King br.	Kingdom xx br.	Kingcraft xx				
			Stute	▲ Norfolk	↑			
		Seenelke	Seeräuber II schw.	Pandur				
			Stute	☦ Nordstern				
Rebanja dbr.	**Kirkland** br. / dbr.	∎ King br.	Kingdom xx br.	Kingcraft xx				
			Stute	▲ Norfolk	↑			
		Stute	Nordland F.	Nobleman	▲		☦	
			Undine	Uncas	↾			
	Stute br.	Norgarth br.	☦ Norval hbr.	▲ Norfolk	+			
			Stute	↾ Hogarth			▲	
		Nuscha	Norderney br.	Nording	☦		↕	
			Weißa	☦ Weißenburg				

Pedigree of Feiner Kerl.

Feiner Kerl (born 1918) was bred in the Verden district, reared at the Herrenhausen court stud, stood at stud for twenty-two years at Altenbruch and sired sixty-one state stallions and over 200 registered mares. The fact that King appears three times in the first four generations of Feiner Kerl's pedigree, and Norfolk eleven times in the fifth to the eighth generations shows that classification according to male bloodlines is of little genetic value, and is merely a formality. The pedigree of the principal representative of the 'F-line' contains only two references to the stallion Flick, the so-called founder of the line! With fifty-three of his male progeny standing at stud in other German breeding zones, Feiner Kerl had a more widespread influence on German horse breeding in the period 1930–1960 than any other warmblood stallion. He is described as broad, deep, compact and very muscular, with a very expressive head, a powerful neck, a rather straight shoulder, a poor saddle area, rather straight hind legs and an energetic, correct action.

Flavius was bred and reared at Herrenhausen and stood at stud from 1918 to 1935 at the Drochtersen stallion station, where he produced twenty-eight Hanoverian state stallions and 125 registered mares. Norfolk appears seven times in the background of his pedigree. He had a common head and was primarily a sire of farm horses. Of the ten state stallions which he sired, Flügelmann I (1933–1949) was the most prepotent. Thanks to his very energetic paces, which were mostly inherited by his descendants, his line still survives today.

21.2 / **187** / **173/163** / **geb. 1915 dbr.** — **Flavius**	**Fling** — Flingarth	Flenheim	■Flick		
			Blüthe	Blenheim xx	
		Kimbale	/King	St. v. ●Nf.	
			Hospodella	Hospodar	
	Kilbe	King	Kingdom xx		
			—	●Norfolk	
		Seenelke	Seeräuber II	●Nf.	
			—	▲Nordstern □E.	
Aurelie	Athanas	Altheo	Alnok	*Adeptus xx u. ▲N.-St.	
			Theorbe	Theorist xx	
		Aduka	Adanus	*Adeptus xx	
			—	Juwelier	
	Cornelie	Cornelius	Colorado		
			—	△Weißenburg ●Nf.	
		Caravella	Carabinier xx	Petronel xx	
			Miller ●Nf.		

Pedigree of Flavius.

Feiertag III by Feiner Kerl, state stallion at Celle 1941–1959.

When the *Verband Hannoverscher Warmblutzüchter* was formed in 1922, a new breeding policy was formulated. The aim was now to breed: 'A warmblood horse with as much substance as possible, which can undertake any type of farm work, but which has enough "blood" and courage, and good enough paces, to make a riding and driving horse of substance.' During the period between the two world wars, the Hanoverian was not a pure 'agricultural warmblood'. After the First World War, Gustav Rau was responsible for fostering an interest in riding among the rural community, including that of the Hanover region. As a result of this, many breeders' sons became keen on riding. During this period many a broodmare was kept who was not actually needed on the farm, but provided a mount for the farmer's son at the local show on a Sunday or an afternoon off. In this way equestrian sport began to spread from the small circle of officers and well-to-do people into the farming community.

In fact the Hanoverian Warmblood was not just a riding horse, but a good one. It distinguished itself in both national and international competitions during the period 1920–1940, as we shall see in a later chapter of this book.

A succession of Thoroughbred stallions, mainly from the Prussian studs of Graditz and Altefeld, ensured that the level of 'blood' in the Hanoverian was maintained. Aberglaube XX by Dark Ronald, Colleoni XX by Aberglaube, Cherusker XX by Nuage, Da Capo XX by Dark Ronald, Ecco XX by Gulliver II, Christian de Wet XX by Gallinule, and Impressionist XX by Prunus are just a few of these.

In the mid 1920s, a new stallion appeared on the scene and founded a new sire line. He came from the Devils Own line, which had been in existence since 1900. He was the chestnut Detektiv (born 1922), by Desmond out of a mare by Khedive. Devils Own XX appears twice in the fourth generation of his pedigree, and Norfolk, as usual, features prominently in the earlier generations. He stood at stud at Drochtersen from 1926 to 1943, and through his sons Dolman and Dwinger, and his grandsons Dollart and especially Duellant, he passed on his powerful neck, shoulders and croup, and contributed elastic, ground-covering paces to the Hanoverian breed. This contribution has not been matched before or since, and this line has been producing outstanding breeding stock and sport horses since 1930.

Following the overproduction in the early 1920s, the three years before and after 1930 were characterised by a slump in the market caused partly by the surfeit of horses which had been produced and partly by a much freer German economic policy

Detektiv geb. 1922 F. 171/162 189 21.8	Desmond	Defregger	Defilant	*Devil's own xx	
				Lisawetha	Landstreicher xx
			—	Optimist	
				—	●Güstrow
		Jabe	Jasmund	Jasal	
				Normannia	Nordend ■Nord /Nf. u △E.
			Flause	F enheim	▲Flick
				—	●Güstrow
	Kalabaka	Khedive	King	Kingdom xx	
				—	/Norfolk
			Delike	*Devil's own xx	
				Nita	■Y. Nf. /Nf. u. △E.
		Concette	Cornelius	Colorado	
				—	□Weißenburg /Nf.
			Leonessa	Lessing	
				—	Ambos I

Pedigree of Detektiv.

Detektiv by Desmond, state stallion at Celle 1926–1943.

which made it easy to import foreign horses. The drive towards self-sufficiency which began in 1934 and the subsequent expansion of the army under national socialism made horse breeding economically viable again, and the level of breeding stocks rose accordingly.

When the currency was again devalued, at the end of the Second World War, the results were the same as at the end of the First World War twenty-five years previously: there was an over-production of horses, which was then suddenly stemmed by the monetary reform in 1948. The fall in value of the horse during the 1950s and 1960s was on a hitherto unprecedented scale. The reason for this was the rapid advance of mechanisation in industry and agriculture – a factor which had been absent on the previous occasion.

Within a decade it had become apparent that these two branches of the economy could now manage without horses, and that the rising cost of labour made it necessary for them to do so. The horse population in West Germany fell to a tenth of its former level. Out of 30,000 registered broodmares in the stud book in 1948, there remained in 1963 a total of 6500, while the number of active stallions fell from 539 to 149! Many of the old, consolidated female lines were lost. On the other hand, the recession actually had a therapeutic effect in that very drastic selection procedures had to be adopted, and consequently only the very best of the stock which remained was used for breeding (i.e. mares and stallions whose progeny would definitely find a market).

This selection, 'from the inside outwards', was one of the pillars upon which the new breeding policy was based. Unlike other German warmblood breeds which consisted of heavy coach horse types, the Hanoverian experienced relatively few problems in the conversion to a riding horse. On the 'inside' of the selection procedure were the stallions from the 'up-grading' breeds – in this case English Thoroughbreds and East Prussian Warmbloods of Trakehner Origin. More use was made of these breeds than previously.

Duellant by Dolman, state stallion at Celle 1946–1965.

45

In the period following the Second World War, the following Thoroughbred stallions in particular made their mark:

ADLERSCHILD XX (1949–63), bay, by Ferro out of a mare by Herold, from the Graditz 'Held' family, which was based on the mare Antwort. There were six state stallions among his progeny, and he also produced eighty-eight registered competition horses who recorded winnings of nearly 300,000 DM.

MARCIO XX (1953–65), bay, by Aventin out of a mare by Janus, from the female line of the Walfried mare Macht. There were six state stallions, almost ninety registered mares and 203 competition horses (whose winnings totalled over 330,000 DM) among his progeny.

DER LÖWE XX (1951–73), bay, by Wahnfried out of a mare by Herold, bred by the Röttgen stud. Six state stallions, 158 registered mares, and 314 competition horses (with winnings of about 750,000 DM) were among his progeny. Der Löwe XX is the most important Thoroughbred stallion in the postwar history of the Hanoverian. By the early 1980s there were ten of his grandsons or great-grandsons at the Celle stud.

(Opposite page)
Marcio XX by Aventin, state stallion at Celle 1953–1965.
Der Löwe XX by Wahnfried, state stallion at Celle 1951–1973.

Adlerschild XX by Ferro, state stallion at Celle 1949–1963.

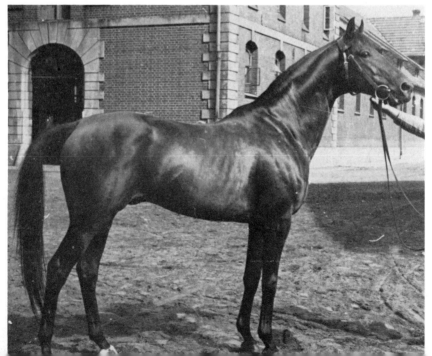

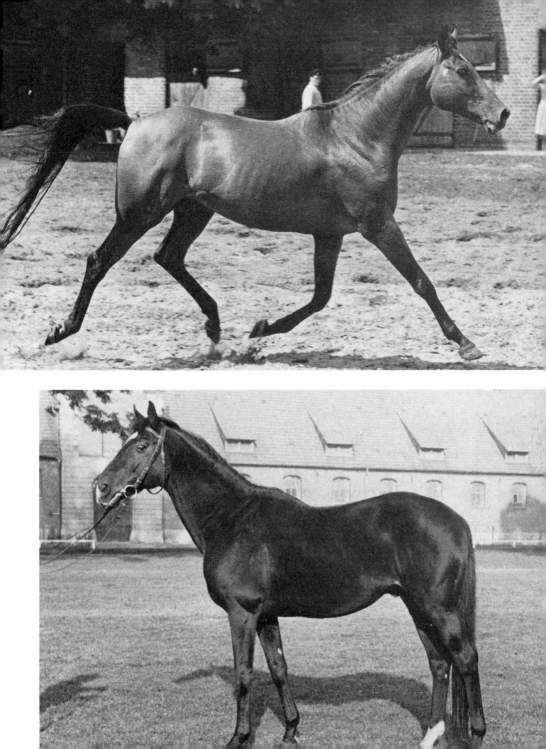

PIK AS XX (1953–69), bay, by Abendfrieden out of a mare by Mirze II, has produced four licensed Hanoverian stallions, plus eighty-two registered mares and 142 competition horses with winnings of well over 450,000 DM. This stallion, who was bred at Mydlinghoven and became famous through the competition successes of his progeny, sired three state stud stallions and is the grandsire of several more.

WAIDMANNSDANK XX (1966–80), black, by Neckar out of a mare by Alchimist, was bred at the Ravensberg Thoroughbred stud. This big horse, with plenty of substance, produced twenty-one graded stallions and 278 registered mares. His progeny also includes several successful Halfbred racehorses, and his dressage and show-jumping progeny have won over 390,000 DM in the arena.

Pik As XX by Abendfrieden, state stallion at Celle 1953–1969.

Waidmannsdank XX by Neckar, state stallion at Celle 1966–1980.

Other Thoroughbred stallions who featured prominently in the post-1960 period of the Hanoverian upgrading programme were:

POET XX (1949–66), chestnut, by Janitor out of a mare by Herold.
JONKHEER XX (1955–69), bay, by Magnat out of a mare by Indus.
NOVUM XX (1967–81), chestnut, by Tabriz out of a mare by Nuvolari.
SUDAN XX (1964–80), bay, by Nizam out of a mare by Arjaman.
STEINPILZ XX (1955–69), bay, by Blasius out of a mare by Janitor.
VALENTINO XX (1957–68), chestnut, by Nuvolari, out of a mare by Abendfrieden.

In the period 1945–1950, the proportion of Thoroughbred stallions stood at 1.8 per cent of the total stallion population, which was the lowest figure ever in the history of the breed. In 1965, of the 160 stallions based at Celle for use in the Hanoverian

49

breeding programme, eleven (6.9 per cent) were Thoroughbreds, and in 1975 this figure had risen to 11 per cent, that is, twenty-three of the 208 state stallions were Thoroughbreds.

Between 1968 and 1977 in particular, there was a strong tendency among breeders to use Thoroughbred stallions because they produced what the buyers wanted. In the following five years the demand for Thoroughbred stallions fell sharply. The breed authorities, who had considered it necessary to call a halt to the use of Thoroughbred blood, are now encouraging the use of good Thoroughbred stallions on suitable mares on the grounds that it is not possible to keep breeding performance horses in the long term without repeated infusions of Thoroughbred blood, though this must be in controlled doses.

As has already been discussed, strictly controlled doses of East Prussian blood (through the use of warmblood stallions of Trakehner origin – now commonly known as Trakehners) had been integrated into the Hanoverian breeding programme as far back as the 1880s. In 1945, when this breed was evacuated from its homeland, some quality East Prussian state stallions found their way to Hanover. They were not used as much as they might have been, because it did not seem at the time that there would ever again be a market for riding horses. A few of them, however, did manage to gain a foothold in some of the principal breeding zones, and to exert considerable influence:

SEMPER IDEM (born Trakehnen 1934), chestnut, by Dampfross out of a mare by Parsival, stood 1946–51 at Drochtersen. This line survives today through his son Senator (1954–73), who produced fourteen state stallions. His grandsons and great-grandsons are at present in use at stud.

ABGLANZ (born Trakehnen 1942), chestnut, by Termit, out of a mare by Poseidon. He stood from 1946 to 1964 in the breeding zone of Lüneburg and Stade, and sired twelve Hanoverian stallions and sixty-five registered mares. He and his progeny did much to bring about the desired improvement in the head and neck of the Hanoverian. There are well over twenty of his descendants from the male line standing at stud in West Germany, and considerable numbers elsewhere in Europe and North America.

(Opposite page)
Semper Idem by Dampfross, Trakehner, state stallion at Celle 1946–1951.
Abglanz by Termit, Trakehner, state stallion at Celle 1946–1964.

50

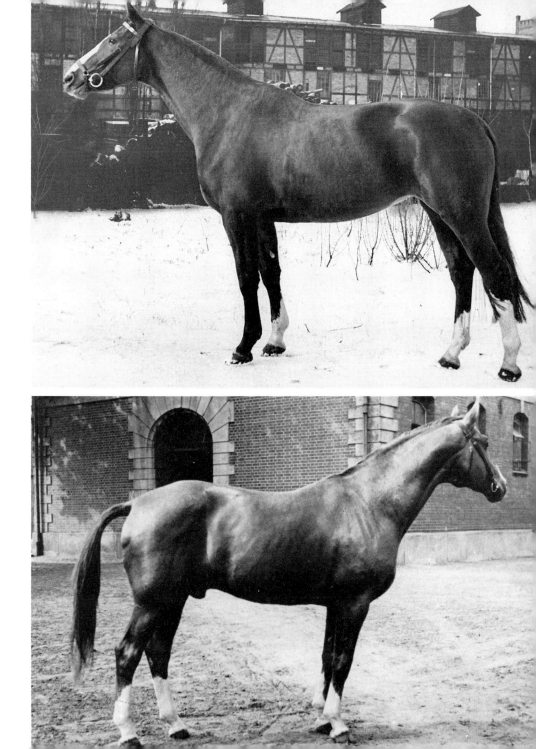

The following Trakehners had less influence on the breeding side, but their progeny distinguished themselves in the sporting field:

LATERAN (born Trakehnen 1942), grey, by Helikon out of a mare by Fetysz OX. He produced five Hanoverian state stallions and 123 registered mares.

CYKLON (born Trakehnen 1943), chestnut, by Helikon out of a mare by Landgraf. He stood from 1946 to 1958 and produced five Hanoverian state stallions and forty-eight registered mares.

ABENDSTERN (born Trakehnen 1936), chestnut, by Poseidon out of a mare by Pirol. Stood 1946–61, and produced one Hanoverian state stallion and forty-seven registered mares.

KEITH (born Trakehnen 1941), chestnut, by Pythagoras out of a mare by Ararad. Stood 1946–65 and produced sixty-one registered mares.

When the postwar generation of Trakehners disappeared from the scene, the number of Trakehner stallions standing at stud fell sharply. Whereas between 1946 and 1966 there were on average ten to twelve, since 1970 there have been only one or two per year. The relatively large numbers of horses available with Trakehner sires have succeeded in bringing about the desired aesthetic improvement in the head and neck of the Hanoverian.

The introduction of Arab blood through Amurath I and his progeny proved very successful, and this Arab element was cultivated more and more by Hanoverian breeders in the first three decades of this century. However, the first cross was almost always behind the average Hanoverian in height, frame size and the coveted clearly defined lines, which made it harder to sell. This accounts for the fact that Arab blood has never again achieved the same degree of influence. The most widely used Arabian state stallions were the following:

JASON OX born 1933 at the Weil Arabian stud, grey, by Jasir out of a mare by Dynamit. Stood 1951–53 and produced one state stallion and eighteen registered mares.

KURDE X born 1935 in Poland, grey, by Koheilan I (OX) out of a mare by Bafur (XX). Stood 1949–56, siring six state stallions and fourteen registered mares. [In German pedigrees, X denotes an Anglo-Arab; pub. note.]

SHAGYA XVII–12, born 1918 at the Hungarian central stud at Bábolna, grey, by Shagya XVII out of a Siglavy-Bagdady mare. Stood 1925–36 and produced one state stallion and sixty-one registered mares.

Jason OX by Jasir, state stallion at Celle 1951–1953.

NEROX born 1938 in Sweden, grey, by Nigro out of a mare by Mersuch. Stood 1949–56 and produced twenty-six registered mares.

HASSAN born Holstein 1941, bay by Hazard OX, out of an Amurath-Sahib mare. Stood 1955–69 and produced two state stallions and fifty-seven registered mares.

Although modern warmblood breeders are not at all keen to keep a direct Arab/Hanoverian cross, they are often delighted if they find an Arabian stallion in the second or earlier generation of the pedigree of one of their mares.

The old Hanoverian bloodlines of Norfolk, Schlütter, Nelusko, Jason and Kingdom XX are now extinct, but those of Adeptus XX–Alderman I, Flick–Flingarth, Goldschaum XX–Goldschläger and Devils Own XX–Detektiv are still in existence. In the 199 stallions who stood at stud in 1982, the bloodlines were distributed as follows:

Goldschläger–Goldfisch II	29	14.5%
Flick–Flingarth	25	12.5%
Abglanz	19	9.5%
Devils Own XX–Detektiv	17	8.5%
Der Löwe XX	13	6.5%
Adeptus XX–Alderman I	10	5.0%
Waidmannsdank XX	7	3.5%
Semper Idem–Senator	6	3.0%
others	73	37.0%

The fact that the Flingarth line lies in second place, 120 years after the period in which its founder was active, can be attributed to the show-jumping successes of his descendants. The two stallions, Ferdinand by Ferrara (a great-grandson of Feiner Kerl) who stood from 1944 to 1967, and Gotthard, were show-jumping sires whose descendants won in every jumping arena in Europe in the 1960s, 1970s and 1980s. The Ferdinand line has been carried on almost entirely by three of his sons: Winnetou, Wedekind and Wendekreis, and the use of frozen semen from these stallions means that their progeny will still be competing for many years to come.

The male descendants of Abglanz are on the increase via his son Absatz, and the latter's sons and grandsons, who are particularly popular outside West Germany. The D-line is represented via Detektiv's grandsons Duellant and Dollart. Among the descendants of these two stallions are most of the top (premium winning) breeding stock, including Dominik, Duft II, Diplomat, Darwin, Dirk and Darling, who are all DLG (German agricultural show) champions.

The Der Löwe XX sons Lugano I and Lugano II were the original pillars of his promising line, which already has more representatives than the highly esteemed, 100-year-old Adeptus line. By 1982 this line rested chiefly on the stallions Eisenherz I by Einglas, the Eisenherz son Eiger I, and Einblick by Eindruck II, although Eisenherz I's popularity as a broodmare sire has led to a partial revival of its influence through the bottom half of the pedigree.

54

Diplomat by Duft I out of a mare by Senator, born 1963, bred by G. Heins of Altenbruch, near Cuxhaven, and reared by the Hunnesrück stallion rearing station in Solling. Champion stallion in the 'German Riding Horse' category at the DLG show in Hanover, 1972.

Waidmannsdank XX by Neckar out of an Alchimist mare is well represented by his sons Waldhorn, Waldmeister and Waidwerk. The Semper Idem line, which has already been discussed, was strong at first, but its numbers have now dropped.

Numerous other genes and combinations of genes are available to the modern breeder in the seventy-three stallions which come under the heading of 'others'. There is far more choice than, for example, in the years 1927 to 1934. During this period, on average, 57 per cent of the stallions belonged to one of two lines – the Flingarth line or the Adeptus line; 21.3 per cent were divided among six other well-known lines; and only 22 per cent fell into the category of 'others'.

The present Hanoverian breeding policy aims to produce: 'A high-class, correct warmblood horse with clearly defined lines, with a capacity for performance, and dynamic ground-covering, elastic paces; a horse which is suitable for any equestrian discipline on account of its temperament, nature and "rideability".'

For the first time in its history, the Hanoverian is almost exclusively a riding horse. It is based partly on bloodlines which can be traced back into the eighteenth century, and whose representatives were neither pure farm horses nor pure riding horses. The development of the breed was greatly influenced by the fact that it was required to produce horses for the army and for use as high-class carriage horses.

The conversion of the Hanoverian in the post-1960 period to a pure riding horse has resulted in the development of a warmblood horse which is based on the old, selected bloodlines but has been adapted to meet market demands through heavy infusions of English Thoroughbred blood, controlled doses of Trakehner blood, and very small infusions of Arab blood.

In the 130-odd years of its existence as a breed in its own right, the Hanoverian halfbred – known since 1921 as a 'warmblood' – has never been a closed shop. Over this period, breeders have never adhered fixedly to one set aim. In fact they have always tried to avoid uniformity within the breed. Once a sufficiently broad female foundation had been achieved, the breed authorities endeavoured, with the help of Thoroughbred, Trakehner and Arab blood, to match their products to the market demands of each period, i.e. to produce a light or heavy farm-cum-military horse in the early decades of the century, then an all-round competition and leisure horse for the present-day market.

6 The state studs

The 'Landgestüt' Celle

As can be seen from the previous chapter, the development of the Hanoverian would not have been possible without the Celle state stud. From the outset the purpose of this stud has been to support private horse breeding in the region. During the first forty years of its existence it was funded by the king from his personal resources, but it was never run as a royal stud for his personal use.

The stud was housed temporarily in rented stabling at the gate of the capital town of Celle. During the years 1735–1746 land was acquired and buildings erected, and the stud developed into a complex which now covers an area of 7.5 hectares (18.5 acres) within the boundaries of what is now a district town.

The oldest building is the so-called 'Reithausstall' (1774) [2] north of the bridge over the stream known as the Fuhse [3]. The long feed shed dates from the same period [8]. The 'Spörckenstall' [5], the coach house [7] and the indoor school [6] on the east and south sides of the parade ground [18] date from the years 1830–1840. The 'Jägerstall' [1] north of the Fuhse was built around 1880, and the 'Bergstall' [14] as an isolation block on the western boundary in 1897. The 'Grabenseestall' [17], to the west of the parade ground, dates from 1905–1906, and the 'Burgstall' [10] on the southern perimeter from 1912. In 1949 a carriage store [15] was erected parallel to the 'Grabenseestall' and to the west of it. The most recent buildings date from 1974–1975, and are replacements for buildings standing on a piece of land which ceased to be part of the stud in 1962. The new buildings are the forge and the wheelwright's workshop to the north-west of the 'Grabenseestall' [16], a coach house and classrooms as an extension of the open-fronted carriage store, and a block of loose boxes and an official's residence adjoining the 'Burgstall' [11]. Despite the great age of many of the buildings, areas such as the big central arena where the stallion displays are held have an aura of quiet majesty.

In fitting with its purpose, the state stud was designed to be run in close liaison with the farmer-breeders. After the first few years, during which it was treated with the natural suspicion experienced towards a new government department, a relationship built up between breeders and breed authorities, especially over the course of the nineteenth century, which it would have been hard to better. The stud managers, who were experts with practical experience, trod a narrow path between the wishes of the farmers and those of the military authorities, although in essence their work was simply a continuation of that begun by the Spörcken brothers (1816–1866).

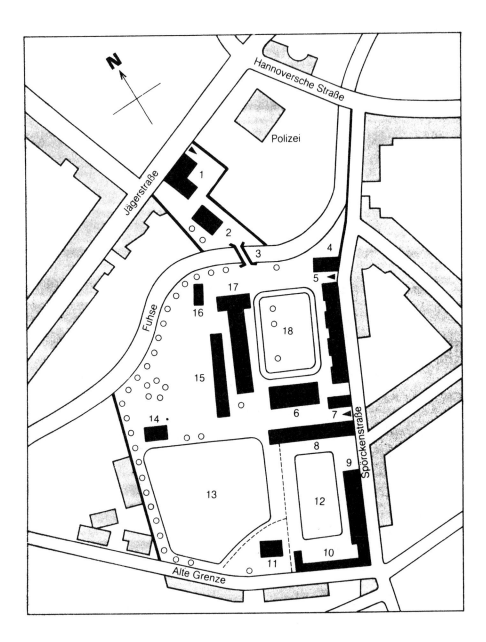

(Opposite page)
Plan of the Celle state stud, 1982.

1. 'Jägerstall'
2. 'Reithausstall'
3. Bridge over the Fuhse
4. Canteen
5. 'Spörckenstall'
6. Indoor school
7. Coach house
8. Feed shed
9. 'Neuer Burgstall'

10. 'Burgstall'
11. Employees' residence
12. 'Kamp' outdoor arena
13. 'Berg' outdoor arena
14. 'Bergstall'
15. Carriage store
16. Workshops
17. 'Grabenseestall'
18. Parade ground (main arena)

The 'Spörckenstall' at the Celle state stud, built *c.* 1840.

There was close liaison between the state stud and the districts it served. This liaison was achieved mainly through the managers of the individual stallion stations. In the eighteenth century the latter were simply known as 'stallion lads' (*Beschälknechte*), but during the nineteenth century they received the official title of *Deckstellenvorsteher* or *Stationsvorsteher* (manager). Not until the end of the First World War did they become *Landesbeamte* (civil servants). Right up until about 1950, 80 per cent of all stud managers came from small farms in the Hanover region, most of which also bred horses. The fact that he came from a farming background, had received an intensive training in horse management, riding and driving (military service in the cavalry was a point of honour), and had gained experience at various different stallion stations made the *Gestüter*, as he was nicknamed, the local adviser on matters of breeding and selling. The highest ranking official in Prussian horse breeding, *Oberlandstallmeister* Duke Georg Lehndorff, was led to comment to Dr Grabensee, *Landstallmeister* of Celle, that the state stud managers were an elite corps.

Nowadays, young people wishing to take up stud management as a career are interviewed and given a riding test at the end of their secondary school education and taken on at the state stud as trainees. The two- or three-year training period, which is spent at the stallion testing centre, ends with the *Pferdewirt* examination. If students then wish to have further training, and the stud is in agreement, they undergo an additional period of practical and theoretical training in the handling of stallions during the stud season and in riding and driving. They then join the workforce of the stud, usually after about five years. When they reach the age of twenty-seven, they can be declared a 'life member' of the stud profession. At around this age, occasionally earlier, the young men are given their first stallion stations to run (as yet, women tend not to take up careers in stud management in West Germany). This entails looking after the stallions, practical stud duties during the covering season, filling in stallion returns and foal certificates, correspondence with the central stud and the breed society, handling breeders' visits, branding foals, purchasing feed and bedding, and collecting stud fees and the additional fee payable on the birth of a live foal. In 1982 there were sixty such stations under the control of the main Celle stud.

If the station is run as it should be, work carries on for twelve to fourteen hours a day during the four and a half months from the end of February to the beginning of July. The routine at these stations, which are mostly attached to country inns, has to fit in with the work on the farms. The sixty stations are distributed over the whole of Lower Saxony, with the exception of the Oldenburg zone, and over the Hamburg district. Where, for example in the Verden and Hoya regions, the stallion stations are still attached to inns, their history can be traced back to the eighteenth century. On average there are three stallions at each station, though there may be as few as one or two or, at the big stations, as many as eight.

About half of the new stallions bought each autumn come from the stallion sale at Verden-an-der-Aller. It is to this event that young stallions aged two-and-a-half years are brought to be licensed and sold. The remaining third come from the stallion rearing centre at Hunnesrück.

At the present a total of thirty-two to thirty-six young stallions per year are bought from these two sources and are taken to the stallion testing station at Adelheidsdorf, near Celle, for one year's training leading up to a performance test. In addition to these stallions, every year one or two Thoroughbred stallions which have proven themselves on the racecourse are also purchased, together with the occasional Trakehner or foreign-bred horse.

The Hunnesrück stallion rearing centre

Up until the end of the First World War, the state stud obtained its supplies of new stallions almost exclusively from Mecklenburg and Pomerania. As has already been discussed, large numbers of potential Hanoverian stallions were bought as foals by estate farmers in these regions and then offered for sale again, unlicensed, to the *Landstallmeister* of the Celle stud at the age of two and a half years. Those which did not make the grade went to the army or to farmers.

This was a very good arrangement since it provided an outlet for the foals (the Hanoverian breeders mostly used broodmares for farm work and counted the foals as a cash crop), and the young stallions benefited from the good grazing in Mecklenburg and Pomerania. Many top Hanoverian stallions would not have developed into such quality animals if they had been reared in a less favourable environment.

During the period of high inflation after the First World War, this arrangement ran into severe difficulties. Stallion markets sprang up in Güstrow (Mecklenburg) and Stettin (Pomerania), and foreigners with hard currency had no difficulty in buying up all the best stallions – much to the detriment of the Hanoverian state stud. This made the Prussian breeding authorities decide to set up a stallion rearing centre (*Hengstaufzuchtgestüt*) at Hunnesrück, near Einbeck-am-Solling. The 520 hectare estate had formerly belonged to the church. It passed into state ownership in 1806 and was a Prussian remount depot from 1868 to 1921.

61

Celle stallion display: coach and six-in-hand.

Celle stallion display: Hungarian Post.

Celle stallion display: the dressage quadrille.

displays rather than in competitions. The fast-moving, colourful programme provides the breeder with the information he requires and at the same time provides excitement and entertainment for the horse-loving public. The displays feature a wide range of activities such as a parade of stallions in hand, a six-in-hand driven in a coach (with all concerned in period costume), a dressage quadrille performed by twenty-four stallions, and chariot racing. This annual event is an excellent publicity exercise for the stud.

The 'Landgestüt' Osnabrück

In 1925 a second state stud was established, in the Osnabrück suburb of Eversburg. It was a large establishment with purpose-built facilities, and was responsible for supplying stallions for the administrative districts of Hanover, Osnabrück and

Hildesheim. It was set up with 114 warmblood stallions from Celle together with the appropriate number of staff.

In 1930, ten coldblood stallions were installed at Osnabrück. These were the first ever state stallions of coldblood type. This number subsequently rose, reaching a peak of seventy-six in 1949. During the whole of the stud's thirty-six year history, coldbloods never accounted for more than one-third of the total stallion population. A few Norwegian Fjord stallions stood at this state stud (the Fjord made a good working horse for the small farmer) and small numbers of Oldenburgs and East Friesians were also used.

In spite of bitter opposition from warmblood breeders to the use of coldbloods, they can now be seen to have done little harm to Hanoverian warmblood breeding. In fact they were very useful in that they actually saved many state stallion centres from closing down; the minimum number of stallions per station was two, and when there were not enough warmblood stallions to go round, one of them would be replaced by a coldblood or a Fjord.

The highest number of mares covered by Osnabrück stallions was 15,760, in 1947. In 1960, 1766 mares were covered by seventy-one stallions – twenty-five mares per stallion. That same year the Lower Saxony legislative assembly took the decision to close down the Osnabrück stud at the end of the 1961 stud season and to transfer the stallions, equipment and some of the staff to Celle.

At one time the best quality horses in the Osnabrück zone were bred in Artland, an area of great natural beauty served by the Badbergen stallion station and lying in the north of the present-day Osnabrück district. Later it was the areas served by the Sudweyhe (Bremen), Oiste (Verden) and Hoyerhagen (Hoya) stations on the left bank of the Middle Weser which came to the fore, together with, from 1952, the Thedinghausen area. The Thedinghausen station and the office bearing the same name actually belonged to Brunswick, and had been under the jurisdiction of the former Brunswick state stud at Harzburg until that point.

In the thirty-six years of its existence the Osnabrück state stud had six directors, or *Landstallmeister*. Of these, the last one, Dr Julius Kiel (1945–1961), held office for the longest time and was therefore able to do most to support and consolidate Hanoverian breeding, though without neglecting other forms of breeding.

The 'Landgestüt' Harzburg

In the summer of 1960, one year before the Osnabrück stud at Eversburg was closed down, the Harzburg state stud at Bündheim, on the northern edge of the Harz, was also disbanded. The stock of nine warmblood and twelve coldblood stallions, together with some of the staff, was annexed to the Celle state stud. The Harzburg stud had belonged to Brunswick until 1946 and then to Lower Saxony.

There had been an early form of stud (a reserve on which horses were left to breed naturally) at Bündheim from the middle of the seventeenth century to the beginning of the nineteenth. In 1815, the Duke of Brunswick set up his personal stud there, to which a public stud for the duchy of Brunswick was added in 1824. In 1831 the public section of the stud was moved to the town of Brunswick. It stayed there until 1924, when it was moved back to Bündheim, near Harzburg. In the first half of the nineteenth century the stallion stations of the duchy of Brunswick contained only highly bred stallions such as Hanoverians from the Verden region, East Prussians and Mecklenburgs. The demand for farm horses in the Brunswick area, which consisted predominantly of heavy soils suitable for growing root crops and wheat, soon led to the authorities buying in English draught horses, especially Shires. Before long everyone was crossing carthorse stallions with highly bred mares, which resulted in a terrible hotch-potch. Not until the end of the nineteenth century did they decide to begin pure-breeding, on Belgian foundations, and to keep coldbloods and warmbloods strictly separate. Of the warmblood stallions, Hanoverians were in the majority. In the year 1900, the Harzburg state stud had a total of thirty-nine stallions: twenty coldbloods, ten Hanoverians, one Thoroughbred and eight other warmbloods.

The Thedinghausen office and the stallion station of the same name are situated twenty kilometres south of Bremen in the Weser marshes, and were part of Brunswick until 1975. This station has had Hanoverian or Thoroughbred stallions ever since 1824, and is one of the top Hanoverian breeding zones. In the 1930s the Thedinghausen stud book for warmbloods of the light type (*Thedinghäuser Stutbuch für edles Warmblut*) was incorporated into the Hanoverian studbook.

Over the first six years after Harzburg was taken over by Celle the activities of the other eleven Harzburg stallion stations were concentrated into just two: Cremlingen, near Brunswick, and Rhüden, near Seesen. There are generally about nine stallions at these stations. The breeders from the whole of the former Brunswick area now depend on these two stations. Many of them do not have good facilities for rearing warmbloods, but what they lack in this respect they make up for in enthusiasm and dedication.

7 Privately owned stallions

The Prussian *Oberlandstallmeister*, Duke Georg von Lehndorff (1866–1912), said that the state studs, by making stallions available to private breeders, should show the way to the private horse-breeding industry until such time as they were no longer needed, that is, until under their influence similar animals had been bred at the established private studs.

In Hanover, things happened the other way round, though also with good results. The 35,000 or so broodmares which, according to Schöttler, were in use in the Hanover region in 1830, were said to have been sired mainly by fairly heavy privately owned stallions.

In 1821 the government had already issued a decree concerning privately owned stallions. The main effect of this was to ban the use of stallions as riding animals. In 1844 the first stallion licensing order was passed in Hanover. This resulted in a drop in the number of privately owned stallions. In the years 1850–1860, out of an annual total of 20,000 foals, the proportion sired by private stallions fell from 74 per cent to 62 per cent. In 1880 there were still 185 private stallions standing at stud, in comparison with 199 state-owned stallions. In the same year, the state stallions covered 10,680 mares and the privately owned stallions 12,223 mares. Included in the last figure, however, are mares covered by East Friesian private stallions. The latter always recorded disproportionately high covering figures.

As has already been discussed, between 1880 and 1930 at the urgent request of the administrative authorities and of the agricultural community, more and more stallion stations were set up in non-marshland areas. Horses were bred on the marshes as a commercial proposition, while those in the non-marshland areas were mostly bred for use by the owner on the farm. The last private stallion station in the Stade administrative area, which is the main Hanoverian breeding area, closed down in 1938, and the last one in the Hanover administrative area in 1954.

There are now again over twenty privately owned stallions in the Celle area which are approved, with or without restrictions, for Hanoverian breeding. There are also about sixty further stallions in private hands in the former Oldenburg area which have full or limited approval for use in Hanoverian breeding. These high numbers are due to the boom in riding horse sales between 1972 and 1975. The number of private breeders in West Germany trebled within four years. The fact that more Hanoverian stallions than any other breed were approved for use as Oldenburg sires also helps to explain the large numbers of privately owned Hanoverian stallions.

8 The breed society

In 1922 the *Provinzial-Verbandes Hannoverscher Warmblutzüchter* was established, with its headquarters at the offices of the chamber of agriculture in Hanover. This society replaced the fifty breed societies which existed at the time, and which had a total of 5000 members between them actively engaged in horse breeding. Some of these societies were sixty to seventy years old (e.g. Lüneburg, founded 1854; Verden, founded 1855). The new society was also the legal successor to the *Hannoversche Stutbuchgesellschaft*, which had been founded in 1888. Its aims were to represent the interests of all Hanoverian breeders, to control and evaluate breeding activities from one central standpoint, and to promote the sale of Hanoverian stock. With the fall in the demand for remounts at the end of the First World War, this last function became very important for the future of the breed.

The main elements of the society are the council, at the head of which is a President with two Deputies; the stud-book committee; the annual members' meeting with elected delegates; and the Secretary. All posts except the last one are honorary. The Secretary is responsible for the stud book, marketing, publicity and finance. Affiliated to the society are the Hanoverian riding and driving school (*Hannoversche Reit- und Fahrschule*) in Verden, and the marketing centre (*Absatzzentrum*) in the same town.

The breeders' clubs

As Hanoverian breeding has become established, breeders' clubs, of which there are about fifty at present, have grown up around the state stallion stations. These clubs, together with the managers of the stallion stations, are the actual executive organs of the Hanoverian society. They organise stud-book registrations and the annual mare show in the club's area and discuss with the manager of the state stud which stallions are to stand at their stallion station.

Between the Hanoverian society and the clubs are the district societies, which are based on current, or sometimes former, administrative districts. At present there are eight of these, namely: Stade, Lüneburg, Hanover, Osnabrück, Emsland, East Friesland, South Hanover–Brunswick, and Hamburg.

The stud book

The stud book, now known as the *Zuchtbuch* but previously called the *Stutbuch*, has

been in existence since 1888. The first printed edition was published in 1893. It had
been put together from entries in the covering registers kept by the Celle state stud
since the middle of the nineteenth century. The next editions of the stud book were
published at irregular intervals until 1927, when they began to appear yearly. Lists of
Hanoverian stallions were published by the state stud up until the beginning of the
Second World War. Since 1951, these have been published at intervals of three to
five years by the Hanoverian breed society.

The central stud book in Hanover is kept up to date from the annual registration
applications, most of which have to be sent in May, and from the foal returns sent in
by the private and state stallion stations. The foal certificates, which were introduced

Combined covering certificate and foal birth certificate from 1840.

by the Celle stud in about 1780, are made out by the manager of the stallion station and given to the breeder. In the case of foals sired by approved private stallions, the certificate is made out at the headquarters of the breed society. This document is a covering certificate as well as a birth certificate, and its basic format has remained unchanged since its introduction in about 1780 by Elderhorst, who was manager of Celle at the time. Different colours for different categories have existed since the beginning of the nineteenth century: blue is for the offspring of a Thoroughbred,

Combined covering certificate and foal birth certificate issued by the Royal Prussian stud at Celle in 1915.

(Opposite page)
Computerised foal pedigree and birth certificate, 1982.

Hannover

Leb-Nr.: **31 - 22014-82** DECKSCH.2281014
Deckstelle: WOLTERDINGEN

Aus der Bedeckung der Stute:		vom Hengst:		am:		vom Hengst:		am:		vom Hengst:		am:

DONNA CAMILLA   H316941866   EXPONENT   05.06.81

ist nachfolgendes Fohlen
gefallen: Geb. am: 02.05.82 Geschlecht: STUTE

Züchter:
Eigentümer/   31040032700 SCHROEDER,OTTO,INSEL,STUTENSTR.9,3043 SCHNEVERDINGEN
Besitzer: DERSELBE

Farbe und   DUNKELBRAUN
Abzeichen   ST.,GR.I.BD.NUEST.RCHD.SCHN.,BD.HF.W.----

Vater:	VV			ATHOS (HANN.)	B
	EISENHERZ II	EINGLAS		310324838	
	310420669	310403058		FAKI (HANN.)	R
EXPONENT	(HANN.)	B (HANN.)		H313159638	
317600177		VISION		VALENTINO XX	F
(HANN.)		H316517361		310394250	
	B	F (HANN.)		FUCHSHELDIN (HANN.)	F
				H316225156	
	VM	ADLERFARN II		ADLERSCHILD XX	B
	ALKE	310405360		310367143	
	H317505270	B (HANN.)		ANGLERBAD (HANN.)	F
	(HANN.)			H315218747 ST.PR.	
		ELBHARFE		ERNOE (HANN.)	R
		H316535362		310395954	
	B	F (HANN.)		KONSOLE (HANN.)	R
				H315268248	

Mutter:	MV			DOMINANT (HANN.)	F
	DOBERAN	DOLUS		310338940	
	310395254	310382249		ALLERPOST	
	(HANN.)	F (HANN.)		H312923637 ST.PR.	
DONNA CAMILLA		FREINIXE		FREIWALD (HANN.)	B
H316941866		H315534949 ST.PR.		310362043	
(HANN.)	R	R (HANN.)		SCHWAMONE (HANN.)	B
				H313544340	
	MM	DOMINIKANER III		DOEMITZ I (HANN.)	B
	DICHTERPALME	310399556		310357444	
	H316613062	B (HANN.)		ABENDHEIT (HANN.)	B
	(HANN.)			H313769741 ST.PR.	
		FRIESENFREUNDIN		FRIESLAND (HANN.)	B
		H315843952		310342441	
	R	B (HANN.)		S311833142	
				(HANN.	

und 9 weitere Generationen

Hannover

Gebrannt am ....07.06.1982....

gez.Dittmer
Fohlenbrand (linker Hinterschenkel)

Eintragungsbrand und Stutbucheintragung
siehe Rückseite)

Weitere Abstammungen der mütterlichen
Vorfahren:

BAND 28

i.A. Piehler
(Stutbuchführer)

Vorstehende Angaben werden hiermit bestätigt:

Hannover, den   25/06/82

pink for the offspring of a warmblood, and white for a foal out of an unregistered mare. After a great deal of preparatory work, the early 1980s saw certificates for foals by state stallions starting to be drawn up by computer, and the system is now completely computerised, along with the mare and stallion returns.

Conditions for registration in the Hanoverian stud book have gradually become more and more strict. For the first thirty years the following applied: 'To be eligible for registration in the stud book, the mare must be free from hereditary defect, and, as well as her sire, the sire of her dam and the sire of her granddam must be shown to be of homogenous descent.' In 1923 the requirement was increased from a three- to a four-generation pedigree on the male side, and the dam of the applicant had to be already registered in the stud book.

For mares whose dams were not registered and which had only a two- or three-generation pedigree on the male side, an appendix to the stud book (*Stutbuchanhang*) was introduced. In 1946 a third section was introduced, the *Vorbuch*, which was for mares in the warmblood category sired by approved pedigree stallions.

These three sections later came to be known as the *Hauptstutbuch* (Main Studbook), *Stammbuch* (Studbook), and *Vorbuch* (Preliminary Book). In 1966, the name of the *Stammbuch* was changed to *Stutbuch*. In 1978 another register, the so-called *Vorbuch 2*, was started for mares without pedigrees but of the light warmblood type. The current requirements for registration are as follows:

HAUPTSTUTBUCH (Main Studbook). The following are eligible: mares of three years and older, out of dams registered in the Studbook or Main Studbook. The sire and the sires of the dam, the granddam and the great-granddam on the female side must be able to prove descent from stallions recognised by the Hanoverian stud book (four-generation pedigree).

STUTBUCH (Studbook). The following are eligible: mares of three years and older out of registered dams (including dams registered in the *Vorbuch*), and whose sire, dam's sire and granddam's sire on the female side can prove descent from stallions recognised by the Hanoverian stud book (three-generation pedigree).

VORBUCH 1 (Preliminary Book 1). The following may be registered: warmblood mares of three years and older with a pedigree certificate from a recognised breed society affiliated to the German equestrian federation ('FN'). Horses must be of the type envisaged in the Hanoverian breeding policy and must satisfy the requirements laid down for conformation. The sire and the sire of the dam must belong to a breed recognised by the Hanoverian stud book.

VORBUCH 2. The following may be registered: mares of three years and older without a pedigree, but which are of the light warmblood type.

Mares of Trakehner, Holstein or Westphalian breeding are accepted provided a pedigree of the number of generations required for the Hanoverian stud book is available. English Thoroughbred mares may be accepted for registration in the Main Studbook if they are above average as regards frame size, height, presence, correctness and action.

The progeny of the non-Hanoverian dams described above can only be accepted for registration in the Hanoverian stud book if the sire is a branded Hanoverian stallion.

Brands indicating registration in the Hanoverian stud book are on the left hand side of the neck as illustrated. A foal may only be branded in its first year if it is still with its dam. The foal is hot-branded on the left thigh and provided that at the time of its conception its sire was a stallion recognised by the Hanoverian society, is given the same brand that its dam received on the left side of her neck when she was accepted for registration in the stud book. In the 1980s a number brand on the neck was introduced, given at the same time as the foal brand on the left thigh.

The stallion registration requirements are even stricter. Even before the days of the stud book, the Celle stud would only use stallions which had a pedigree going back several generations. From 1892, a full four generations were required, and in 1946, when the *Vorbuch* was introduced, the requirement was increased to six generations.

At present the following conditions must be met for the stallions to be recognised: the sire of the stallion and the sires of his five female ancestors in the direct female line must be recognised by the Hanoverian stud book (i.e. a total of six generations). In addition, the dam and her dam must be Hanoverian *Hauptstutbuch* (Main Studbook) mares, but it is sufficient for the great-granddam on the dam's side to be registered only in the *Stutbuch* (Studbook).

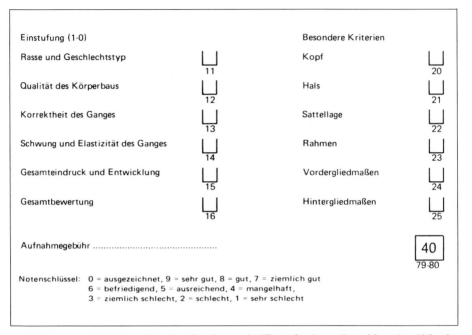

Assessment form for registration. Grading marks (*Einstufung*) are allotted from 1 to 10 for the six specific conformation points (*Besondere Kriterien*) on the right-hand side of the form: head (*Kopf*), neck (*Hals*), saddle position (*Sattellage*), frame (*Rahmen*), forelegs (*Vordergliedmassen*), hindlegs (*Hintergliedmassen*). The total of these six marks is divided by 6, and this average is entered in the left-hand column in the box labelled quality of conformation (*Qualität des Körperbaus*). Grading marks are then given for the other criteria: breed and gender type (*Rasse und Geschlechtstyp*), correctness of gaits (*Korrektheit des Ganges*), swing and elasticity of gaits (*Schwung und Elastizität des Ganges*) and general impression and development (*Gesamteindruck und Entwicklung*). The left-hand column is then totalled and divided by 5, and this is the overall assessment mark (*Gesamtbewertung*). Marks are awarded throughout on the following scale (*Notenschlüssel*): 10 = excellent, 9 = very good, 8 = good, 7 = fairly good, 6 = satisfactory, 5 = sufficient, 4 = insufficient, 3 = fairly poor, 2 = poor, 1 = very poor. The overall assessment mark decides the actual grading category (*Aufnahmegebühr*) of the animal concerned.

80

When a mare or stallion is registered, a form is immediately filled in, describing in an abbreviated form the main characteristics of the conformation and the height and the weight (light, medium or heavy). This form serves as a record for breeding purposes.

Since 1975 marks have been allocated from one to ten, as on the form reproduced on the opposite page. On the right-hand side of the form are six points relating to conformation. The marks for these are added up and divided by six, and the total entered in the box as 'Quality of conformation' (*Qualität des Körperbaus*). The 'Overall assessment' (*Gesamtbewertung*) mark is arrived at by adding up the marks in the five boxes above and dividing by five. A mare needs a minimum mark of six to be accepted for registration in the *Hauptstutbuch* (Main Studbook). A stallion requires a minimum mark of seven to be accepted provisionally (final acceptance depends on the successful outcome of the performance test).

The number of live registered mares rose from a mere 6000 or so in 1961 to 11,305 in 1974 and over 16,500 in the early 1980s. This figure makes the Hanoverian breeding industry the largest organised riding horse breeding industry in Europe, with over 2000 mares being registered each year, of whom approximately 80 per cent will have been accepted in the *Hauptstutbuch* (Main Studbook), with the remainder registered in the other three sections. Interestingly of the mares *covered* in 1976, 88 per cent were registered in the stud book, but by 1981 the proportion had risen to 94.3 per cent. This trend towards organised breeding has now been in evidence for some time and is a sign that non-farming breeders, who have been on the increase over recent years, are also being well served by the breed society.

Shows, premiums and performance testing

Mare shows and the awarding of premiums have been and are still some of the most important promotional measures in modern horse breeding. As early as 1834 the Celle state stud was holding premium shows for mares and foals sired by state stallions in conjunction with Thoroughbred and Halfbred racing, for which a race-course had been constructed at Celle.

The first mare show held along modern lines took place in Otterndorf on the Lower Elbe in 1846. This was followed seven years later by shows in Stade, Lüneburg and Nienburg. Money prizes and certificates were given out, and the owners of prize-winning mares had to undertake to use the mare for breeding, otherwise the prize money had to be repaid. In 1879 the agricultural associations took over the running of these shows from the Celle state stud.

81

Premium certificate from 1890.

In 1888, when the Hanoverian stud book was founded, new rules were drawn up for foal and mare shows and for the awarding of premiums, and these have formed the basis for the present-day rules. Up until 1939, two grades of show were provided for. Grade I shows were held mainly in the marshland districts and were for mares from old bloodlines. Grade II shows were held in non-marshland areas and were for the mares with the shorter pedigrees. In time, Grade II shows were able to advance to Grade I.

From 1935 to 1939 there were the same number of shows in each grade. From 1939 onwards, only Grade I shows were held, and their rules were roughly the same as they are today. The current rules state that the following mares are eligible to take part:

Section 1: Two-year-old mares whose pedigrees make them eligible for registration in the Main Studbook.
Section 2: Three-year-old Main Studbook mares.
Section 3: Four-year-old Main Studbook mares.
Section 4: Five- and six-year old Main Studbook mares, who must have had at least one foal.

Approximately 10 to 15 per cent of newly registered three-year-old mares are

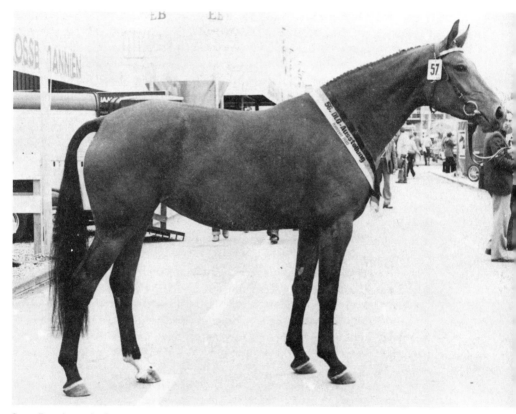

State Premium-winning mare Ascona, by Argentan out of a mare by Seefischer. Bred by J. Tobaben, Ottensen. Champion German Riding Horse mare at the DLG show, Hanover 1980.

awarded government premiums at the annual mare shows. The 1982 value of the premiums was 800 DM. Only mares which are classified as above average are awarded premiums. The breed society has the right to purchase any colt foals from the mare and the owner has to undertake to use the mare to whom the premium has been awarded for breeding for a period of three years, to send her only to a recognised stallion, not to sell her without a permit, and to take her to shows during this period. The money cannot be paid, and the mare cannot be registered as a State-Premium winning mare, until she has passed an eighteen-day performance test aimed at assessing her suitability for riding.

The President of the breed society or his Deputy, the society's breeding activities director and the Director (*Landstallmeister*) of the state stud generally act as judges at the mare shows, which take place every year in June and July at fifty-five different locations at present. The judges are looking for: an expressive head, well set on neck without thickness through the throat, plenty of shoulder and a good saddle position, a swinging back, a long, muscular croup, plenty of depth through the girth, a rounded rib-cage, correct, clean limbs with broad joints, flexible pasterns, a ground-covering, correct, 'light-footed' action, good sexual 'type', and a normal, healthy constitution.

The mare's suitability for producing riding horses is also assessed. However, with 2700 to 3000 mares coming before the judges each year, it would be too time-consuming and expensive to judge all the horses aged three years or more under saddle and so to assess their willingness and suitability in the various fields of activity.

The idea of performance testing originated in the first half of the nineteenth century. The fame of the English Thoroughbred, which owed its very existence to performance testing on the racecourse, led the state stud in conjunction with the *Hannover–Braunschweig–Oldenburgischen Verein zur Verbesserung inländischer Pferdezucht* to construct a racecourse and training centre at Celle in 1834. This *Verein* was a society aimed at promoting the breeding of native horses. Races for Halfbreds as well as Thoroughbreds took place on this course for thirty years, during which time it began to be realised that racing was far too restricted a form of testing to be suitable for the sires of army- and farm-horses alike. The performance testing for stallions which was therefore developed at Westercelle and Adelheidsdorf has been discussed earlier.

As long as horses were being used in agriculture and industry, the daily use of the mare around the farm by the breeder was an excellent indication of her willingness and stamina. In the 1930s it became possible for the first time to performance-test mares on a voluntary basis. However, these tests were only designed to test the draught capabilities of the mare, and although they were a good idea for those regions which bred horses only for use in industry and agriculture, they never caught on in the Hanover region.

In the 1950s the breed society decided to make the awarding of government premiums conditional on passing a draught test. This test consisted in pulling, in single harness, a sledge with a resistance equivalent to a rolling weight of 2500 kg. A distance of 1000 m had to be covered in twelve and a half minutes, and the horse had to stop and restart once during this period. The dams of potential stallions also had to meet this requirement before their offspring could be licensed for use at stud. From the early 1970s, as an alternative to this draught test, premium mares were able to take a ridden test based on a minimum standard in each gait. The mare had to cover 300 m in walk, 750 m in trot, and 1500 m in canter in three minutes (each), and these minimum requirement tests for broodmares were included in the German national competition rulebook (*Leistungsprüfungsordnung* or *LPO*). However, this has now been superceded by the much more thorough eighteen-day performance test for mares which is mandatory for all new Hanoverian premium mares.

Stallion licensing and approval

The oldest licensing order in what is now the Hanoverian breeding zone dates from 1715 and was issued in Harlingerland in East Friesland. In 1821 an official test was introduced for privately owned stallions in the Stade district. The licensing order covering the whole of the Kingdom of Hanover was passed in 1844, and its requirements made stricter in 1860. To be approved for use at stud in the main breeding zones, apart from correct conformation and good paces, the stallion had to be able to prove at least three generations of 'homogeneous, good descent'.

It was the 1892 order which laid down the pedigree requirements in more or less the same form as we know them today. The section on 'keeping the stud book' specifies a six-generation pedigree, which is still a requirement today for stallions in use as sires in Hanoverian breeding.

Of great importance for the Hanoverian breeding zone were the central licensing establishment and stallion market, established in Demmin, Western Pomerania, in 1919 and moved to Stettin in 1931; and the similar establishment in Güstrow, Mecklenburg. Up until 1945 there were few privately owned horse rearing centres in the Hanover region. During the Second World War the boom in the export of young stallions to the eastern territories led to the setting up of a central stallion licensing establishment and stallion market in Bremervörde, in the administrative district of Stade. In 1946, the centre was moved to Verden-an-der-Aller, where it is still based today. When the Pomeranian and Mecklenburg rearing centres were lost, the Hanoverian stallion licensing and sale in Verden became, along with the stallion rearing centre at Hunnesrück, the most important source of young stallions for use in state studs.

In the meantime a private stallion rearing industry has become established in the Hanover zone, mainly in the low-lying grassland areas. This industry has based itself on the experiences of the former remount dealers. The colt foals are either homebred or bought in, and are kept until they are two and a half years old.

Although the period from 1954 to 1965 was a difficult one for the stallion rearing industry, because only limited supplies were required by the state studs and outside buyers were very thin on the ground, a small, enthusiastic group of breeders refused to allow itself to become disheartened. Every year about thirty to forty young stallions, after a preliminary inspection, were brought before the licensing authorities. Barely 50 per cent were accepted, and eight to ten of these were bought in by the stud authorities.

As the demand for riding horses slowly began to grow at the end of the 1960s, the number of young stallions placed at rearing centres, presented for licensing, approved, and sold for use at stud began to rise. In the late 1970s and early 1980s, between 380 and 415 young stallions per year came before the selection committee for the preliminary inspection. Between ninety and one hundred attended the licensing, and about sixty-five to seventy were accepted. The figures for the 1981 licensing, which took place in the licensing area of the Verden marketing centre, are typical, and are as follows:

Young stallions which came before the preliminary selection committee	415
Stallions entered in the licensing catalogue	100
Stallions presented for licensing	96
Stallions licensed	69
Stallions not licensed	27
Stallions sold as licensed for use at stud	
to the Celle state stud, Lower Saxony	26
to other West German state studs	4
to private studs in West Germany	13
to other European countries	9
overseas	5

The young stallions are sold by negotiation through the breed society. Before selling begins, the Celle state stud, as the main Hanoverian stud in the breed's homeland, is allowed to select a number of young stallions (usually about ten) and, with the owners' consent, withdraw them from public sale.

Since 1975 the state stud has had the means available to buy in each year a batch of about thirty-six young stallions. Two-thirds of these come from Verden and one-third from Hunnesrück. This means that there are plenty of stallions to choose from at the end of the twelve months' training at the Adelheidsdorf stallion testing centre, and only those whose marks are above the statistical mean for the group are finally selected for use at stud.

Since 1975 it has been compulsory, according to the provisions of the *Tierzuchtgesetz* (Animal Breeding Act), for all stallions in West Germany intended for use as riding horse sires to undergo at least 100 days' assessment followed by performance testing in the various different disciplines. In this way they prove their suitability as riding horses. The assessment and testing must take place at an approved testing centre.

A horse is considered to have passed the test if its total mark is not more than one and a half points below the average mark for the group. The *Verband Hannoverscher Warmblutzüchter* requires a higher standard than the legal minimum. For approval, a stallion needs to attain a mark not more than one point below the average for the group.

For a stallion to be licensed for use at stud, it needs to pass both elements of the licensing: the inspection at the age of two and a half years, and the performance testing which normally takes place a year later. The inspection which comprises the first part of the licensing examination takes the same form as the mare inspections which precede registration in the stud book, that is, it provides an assessment of the conformation and paces. However, for stallions the pass mark is 7.

Marketing

One of the main reasons for the setting up of the breed society in 1922 was to solve the problem of how to sell the youngstock which was surplus to the breeders' working horse and broodmare requirements without losing money. Up until then, there had been no problems in disposing of this stock, because the army had bought it, but nobody knew what the future held. Between 1880 and 1913 about 1100 to 1250 remounts per year were sold at fifty sales in the Hanover region. In addition to these, about the same number of Hanoverian remounts were bought by the army from the territories east of the Elbe, where they had been taken to be reared after being sold as foals. In the year 1900, a remount fetched about 830 Gold Marks, and in 1913 about 1300 Gold Marks. If this is converted into modern currency, an unbroken three-year-old for use as an army horse was valued at about £8000 or $12,000.

In 1923, when the Reichsmark had been stabilised, the army (the so-called 'hundred-thousand-man army' which existed at that time) again began buying in limited numbers of remounts. The number of sales and of horses sold fell by half, but rose again when the army expanded in 1935. In the Hanover region alone, 2154 remounts were sold in 1938. Hence the army again became the main outlet for Hanoverian youngstock.

Between the two wars, attempts were made in Berlin, Krefeld, Dresden and certain other German cities to hold auctions of Hanoverian riding horses, but these were not successful in the long term because the circle of potential buyers was relatively small.

By 1948 the times were past when every horse could be found a buyer or exchanged against something useful, and the outlook was bleak for those Hanoverians which could not be sold. In the majority of cases, slaughter was the only solution. Then another door opened: the Swiss cavalry had bought horses from Germany, most of which were Hanoverians, during the period 1875–1913. The horses were bought as remounts for the militia-dragoon regiments. These purchases had ceased in the period between the two wars, but in 1948 the Swiss army and the *Verband Hannoverscher Warmblutzüchter* entered into an agreement over the supply of military remounts. This contract was a godsend to the Hanoverian breeding industry, which was suffering badly from the effects of the recession. First, it enabled the breeders to off-load their surplus stock without having recourse to slaughter. Secondly, at a time when selection criteria were based wholly on agricultural use, the minimum standards imposed by the Swiss army for riding qualities helped to preserve the courage and 'breeding' of the Hanoverian.

Sales to Switzerland reached a maximum of 838 in 1951, and ceased when the dragoon regiments were finally disbanded in 1970, with a total of 7146 remounts changing hands in this way.

The year 1949 marked the birth of an event, organised by the breed society, which was to develop over the decades that followed into a sale of international repute: the Verden Riding Horse Auction. At the first sale, eighteen horses were sold at an average price of 1900 DM. The sale took place outside because there was no indoor arena available. From 1950 onwards, two auctions were held per year, one in April and one in October. In 1950, fifty-four horses were sold at an average price of 1947 DM.

Since the early 1950s the Verden auctions have been organised according to the instructions of the society which were originally laid down by the late H. J. Köhler. The horses are carefully selected in accordance with market demands (which are assessed by market research), professionally trained for four to six weeks, and are available for trial by potential purchasers. The setting for the sale is also particularly attractive. It is for these reasons that the sale, which was often beset with problems in early years, has developed in the 1970s and 1980s into an important event in the equestrian calendar both in Germany and abroad.

The first sales were held at a barracks in Verden, but in the early 1950s they moved to the 'Niedersachsenhalle' attached to the *Hannoversche Reit- und Fahrschule* (Hanoverian Riding and Driving School). The latter had been set up in 1948 by the breed society with the aim of reviving riding in the rural community and as a medium for marketing Hanoverian horses.

With the upsurge in riding, and the resulting demand for riding horses, the facilities at this school became inadequate, and the society decided to construct a purpose-built marketing centre with stabling, an auction hall, indoor schools and an administrative block. Every Hanoverian mare owner made a contribution to this marketing centre, which was also subsidised from public funds.

It stands on the edge of the Verden racecourse, and was opened in 1972. The open land around the racecourse also provides an ideal training facility. A contribution to the running costs of this impressive complex is made by the Hanover area cattle- and pig-breeding societies, which make use of the stabling and auction hall facilities. The Training and Marketing Centre (*Ausbildungs- und Absatzzentrum* – AAZ) caters for more horses and has better facilities than any other German establishment of its type.

The first riding horse auction took place there in 1972. The table overleaf gives an idea of the outcome of sales between 1949 and 1980.

The five-year intervals between the sales listed contain many annual fluctuations. What the figures do show, however, is the incredible growth in sales figures in the period from 1970 to 1980. The number of horses sold was doubled, and yet the average price of each horse still rose by 4000 DM.

Foreign buyers have always been welcome. In recent years their numbers have increased, and buyers from England and the USA in particular have become more numerous. This increased foreign interest is due partly to the society's extensive

Year	No. of horses sold	Average price
1949	18	DM 1900
1950	54	DM 1947
1955	110	DM 2915
1960	122	DM 4840
1965	151	DM 8043
1970	173	DM 11,740
1975	248	DM 15,508
1980	337	DM 15,730

Verden auctions, 1949–1980

publicity programme, and partly to the successes of English and American riders on Hanoverian horses in international competition.

Many horses which have gone on to become famous international competition horses have been sold through the Verden auctions; for example, Simona by Weingeist (ridden by Hartwig Steenken), who won the show-jumping world championship in 1974 and the team gold medal at the 1972 Olympics; Ferdl by Ferdinand (ridden by Alwin Schockemöhle), who won the team gold medal at the 1960 Olympics; and Deister by Diskant (Paul Schockemöhle), who won the 1981 European show-jumping championship.

Although the prices paid for the top horses are rising dramatically and this is obviously to the benefit of the vendors, the breed society is particularly keen to prevent too great upward as well as downward fluctuations in prices, so as not to deter those riders who ride for enjoyment in their spare time and cannot afford to pay inflated prices. The Verden auctions have long served to set the levels of prices throughout the Hanover region and to provide a 'shop window' for the breed.

Every year at the end of August about 130 weanling foals and a limited number of broodmares are also sold by auction at Verden, and at the end of October, after the stallion licensing, the unsuccessful stallions are auctioned off and the successful ones sold by private treaty. The training and marketing centre is an ideal location for all the society's marketing activities.

During the 1970s and 1980s attempts have been made to establish annual sales of foals and young horses in other parts of the Hanover region. The two sales for riding horses and one for foals at the auction centre in Kutenholz (Stade district) and the two auctions held each year at Vechta (Oldenburg) for Oldenburg and Hanoverian horses are examples of these.

9 Influence of the Hanoverian on other breeds

The Hanoverian Warmblood has been in existence for over 100 years, and has thus been able to play an important part in the development of many other light horse breeds.

In Germany it has been used as a means of increasing stamina and hardiness in the Oldenburg and the East Friesian, and to give the East Friesian more substance. It is also worth mentioning that in the period from 1850 to 1880 Hanoverian stallions contributed to the development of the Oldenburg coach horse, which was famous throughout Europe (usually through Graf Wedel, born 1862; Agamemnon, 1863; and Emigrant, 1875). Now, after an intensive upgrading process in Oldenburg, using English Thoroughbred blood, there are more Hanoverians standing as Oldenburg sires than any other breed.

The East Friesian coach horse was also greatly influenced by the Hanoverian. From 1819 to 1903, the Celle state stud had stallion stations in East Friesland, and Hanoverian stallions played a part in the creation of the particularly forward-going East Friesian carriage horse. Since 1975, East Friesland, which is divided into four districts, has been part of the Hanoverian breeding zone.

Mecklenburg, east of the Elbe, did much to influence Hanoverian breeding in the first half of the nineteenth century. After the decline of horse breeding in Mecklenburg the reverse situation came about, and it was Mecklenburg which looked to Hanover (as a sort of 'reservoir' of Mecklenburg blood) to help it revive its horse-breeding industry. In 1895 the aim of the Mecklenburg breeding policy was to produce what was described as a horse of Hanoverian type. Between 1895 and 1945, 70 per cent of the stallions at the Mecklenburg state stud at Redefin were bred in Hanover, and 20 per cent had been bred in Mecklenburg from Hanoverian bloodlines.

Near the Mecklenburg border in the Prussian province of Pomerania (now in East Germany) was a stud which had made a vital contribution to the creation of the Hanoverian horse. The Brook stud, owned by the von Seckendorff family, bred the two foundation stallions Jellachich and Zernebog, whose names can be found in the pedigrees of all modern Hanoverians. In the second half of the nineteenth century the western part of this province in particular, which was a big stock-breeding area, suffered a decline in its horse-breeding industry. Not until 1910 did the Pomeranian breed society lay down a new breed policy which marked the beginning of a revival. The aim was to breed a robust, practical, 'short-legged' warmblood from Hanoverian foundations. Favourable conditions enabled good progress to be made, and in the 1930s and 1940s Pomerania was the foremost breeding zone of Hanoverians outside Hanover. In 1938, of the 216 stallions at the Pomeranian state stud at Labes (which was established in 1879), 95 per cent were Hanoverians or warmbloods of Hanoverian origin bred in Pomerania, and the remaining 5 per cent were Thoroughbreds and East or West Prussians.

The warmblood bred in the Prussian province of Brandenburg (now in East Germany) was also developed from Hanoverian and East Prussian foundations. In 1838, the Brandenburg state stud at Lindenau had 158 stallions, of which 85 traced back to Hanoverian foundations on the male side. The broodmare herd at the Brandenburg central stud at Neustadt-am-Dosse also contained a large proportion of Hanoverian blood.

In Sachsen-Anhalt at the beginning of the 1950s, an experimental herd of purebred Hanoverians was established at the Radegast experimental farm by the director of the animal breeding institute of Halle University. Some very good stock was produced, and at the central stallion licensing held at Güstrow in 1963, of the sixteen stallions accepted eight were the progeny of Radegast stallions. Six of the young stallions had actually been bred at Radegast, which was no mean achievement since there were on average only about sixteen mares at the stud.

From time to time the East German stud authorities now buy individual stallions from the Verden stallion sale.

Since Westphalia began breeding warmbloods on Hanoverian foundations in 1922, large numbers of stallions and mares from Hanover have been used, resulting in the development of an outstanding sport horse. Westphalian horse breeding is now independent and only imports horses from Hanover occasionally.

The horses bred in Hessen were originally coldbloods and Oldenburgs. Trakehner and Holstein stallions were used for a while, but the stallions at the Dillenburg state stud are now mainly Hanoverians. Warmblood breeding in Rhineland-Pfalz and Saarland has followed the same pattern.

In the North Rhine region a small group of the formerly very successful coldblood breeders have succeeded in an incredibly short time in developing a riding horse, through the use of Trakehners and a significant proportion of Hanoverian mares and stallions.

The recently established Bavarian Warmblood breeding industry is based to a large extent on Hanoverian mares and filly foals taken there in the 1960s and 1970s. Most of the stallions used at the Landshut state stud, the Schwaiganger state stud (which replaced Landshut), and the private studs have been Thoroughbreds, Trakehners and Hanoverians (the latter since 1970 in particular).

A good indication of the distribution of the Hanoverian in East and West Germany can be gained from the sales figures for licensed Hanoverian stallions for the thirty-five years following the end of the Second World War:

Westphalia	106
Bavaria	69
Hessen	52
North Rhine	35
Rhineland-Pfalz	28
German Democratic Republic	21
Schleswig-Holstein	6
Württemberg	5
Berlin	2
Hamburg	2

Four times this number of Hanoverian broodmares were sold to these regions during the same period.

An idea of the distribution of the Hanoverian around the world can likewise be gleaned from the sales figures for licensed stallions. The longest standing links are with Sweden, which imported considerable numbers of Hanoverian mares and stallions in the period between the wars. Most of these were bought from the breed authorities. Of the twenty mares which were in use at the Flyinge central stud in 1957, only four did not contain Hanoverian blood. In the period which followed mainly Trakehner blood was used, though Hanoverians were still imported occasionally.

Denmark began breeding sport horses in the 1960s. A mixture of Thoroughbred, Swedish, Holstein, Trakehner and Hanoverian blood is being used to develop the Danish Warmblood horse, with stallions of chiefly Hanoverian bloodlines forming a major percentage of those in the stud book.

The development of warmblood breeding in Belgium, following the rapid decline of the coldblood, was based on the use of Hanoverian Warmbloods and French

Anglo-Normans. The modern Belgian-bred riding horse contains about 65 to 70 per cent Hanoverian blood. The Belgian show jumpers won the team bronze medal at the 1976 Montreal Olympics on Hanoverian-bred horses. Belgium regularly imports more Hanoverian stallions for use in its breeding programme than any other country.

Great Britain has increased its imports of Hanoverian stallions in recent years, following the successes of English show-jumping riders mounted on Hanoverian horses, such as the late Caroline Bradley on Tigre by Widerhall and David Bowen with the Olympic horse Boysie by Ballyboy XX. (The present-day situation in Great Britain is discussed more fully in the final chapter.)

Austria has almost entirely 'bred out' the native element in its warmblood population by extensive crossing with Hanoverian and Trakehner stallions. Hanoverian stallions were used in the state-owned halfbred herd at the Piber/Steiermark Lipizzaner stud. One such stallion was the well-known show-jumping sire Ferdinand, from Celle, who stood at stud there during the last two years of his life. The area with the highest concentration of Hanoverian breeding is Upper Austria. In 1980 the state stud at Stadl-Paura, near Wels, had sixteen warmblood stallions, and of these fifteen were either imported from Hanover or were pure Hanoverians bred in Austria.

Since the mid 1970s, nuclei of Hanoverian breeders have formed in the USA and Canada, for example in the states of New York, North Carolina, Florida, California, Ontario and Alberta. A North American Hanoverian society has been formed. The *Verband Hannoverscher Warmblutzüchter* acts as adviser to this society, which bases its stud book conditions on those in force in Germany. (The continuing development of Hanoverian breeding in the USA is discussed later.) A similar situation exists in New Zealand and Australia. In these two countries, imported Hanoverians are mainly used on Thoroughbred mares.

Since the 1950s, south-west African farmers, mainly of German descent, have been using heavy infusions of Hanoverian blood to obtain a sporting horse from Arab and Thoroughbred stock.

In spite of its enormous indigenous horse population, in the 1960s the Soviet Union set up a state stud in the Königsberg district of East Prussia with two Hanoverian stallions and thirty-three mares. The aim of this stud was to breed show jumpers.

Between 1948 and 1983 the following numbers of stallions were sold by the Hanoverian breed society to foreign buyers:

Belgium	56
Denmark	48
Great Britain	19
Austria	15
Sweden	11
Canada	11
USA	10
Switzerland	10
South-West Africa	9
Argentina	8
Luxemburg	8
The Netherlands	6
Brazil	5
Hungary	5
Czechoslovakia	2
Chile	2
Australia	2
USSR	2
Yugoslavia	2
New Zealand	2
Guatemala	1
Zambia	1
Spain	1
South Africa	1

10 The Hanoverian in sport

The Hanoverian Halfbred racehorse

Halfbred breeding is a branch of Hanoverian breeding which dates back to the beginnings of racing in Germany.

In 1834 at Celle, a racecourse was inaugurated which was the brainchild of the *Verein zur Verbesserung der inländschen Pferdezucht* (Society for the Improvement of Native Horse Breeding). Races were held for Thoroughbreds and Halfbreds, including some which were specifically for three- and four-year-old Halfbreds born and bred in the Hanover region, and other classes for horses owned by Hanoverian farmers and sired by state stallions.

Racing was abandoned at Celle in 1863, but it left behind a rural Halfbred breeding industry which still exists today and which is centred on the districts of Hoya and Verden. Mares born in Hanover from Thoroughbred sires put to warmblood Hanoverian mares were crossed with Thoroughbred stallions, and the same process of using Thoroughbred stallions on part-Thoroughbred mares was repeated for many generations, to give the Hanoverian Halfbred racehorse. This process is a classical example of 'grading up' – in some cases these horses are up to 99 per cent Thoroughbred. In practice the Halfbred is more or less indistinguishable from the Thoroughbred. However, because they grow up on farms and do not as a rule receive the same intensive supplementary feeding as racehorses, they do not go into training until they are three years old. The heyday of the Hanoverian Halfbred was the period from 1870 until 1914, when officers' races, many restricted to Halfbreds, were very common. Nowadays Halfbred racing is still practised on the northern racecourses of Hanover, Bremen and Harzburg.

Halfbred breeding suffered severe set-backs after both the First and the Second World Wars when officers' races were discontinued, and now there are very few breeders and even fewer bloodlines remaining. It is interesting to note that this branch of Hanoverian breeding, which involves rigorous performance testing on the racecourse, has never produced a horse which has gone on to be a warmblood sire or a show jumper.

Competition horses before 1914 and between the wars

A German team, some of whom were mounted on Hanoverians, took part in the

Racing at the Celle racecourse, 1835.

1912 Olympics, which were the first Olympic games in which equestrian sports were included.

The history of equestrian sport in Germany dates from the early years of this century, which is somewhat later than in neighbouring European countries. Only officers and well-to-do civilians could take part in this exclusive sporting activity.

The most successful German horse before the First World War was the mare Pepita (1906) by Colani, bred in the Hanover region by Meyer, at Kehdingbruch in the Lower Elbe district. For many years she remained an exceptional performer in dressage, show jumping and three-day eventing. In 1913 alone she won 9315 Gold Marks in twenty-six competitions. After four years' war service she came back and scored many more notable successes in the early postwar years.

After the war, it was not until 1923 that German riders began to appear again in international competitions. In 1924 Prince Sigmund of Prussia fought off strong competition from Sweden and France to win the advanced dressage class at an international competition in Malmö, Sweden, on the Hanoverian Christoph II by Christian de Wet XX. In 1928, Freiherr von Langen won the Olympic gold medal for dressage in Amsterdam on the Hanoverian Draufgänger by Aldech. Hammer by Hammerschlag XX, ridden by Käthe Franke, was Germany's most successful dressage horse in 1938.

In three-day eventing, the best-known Hanoverians in the period between the wars were Kirklandsenkel by Kiliar, who won the German Olympic Committee's advanced event in 1934, and Leopold by Butcher Bird XX, who won the advanced competition at Insterburg.

It is in international show-jumping that the Hanoverian has attained the highest distinction. Right back in 1924, Apoll by Defilant, ridden by Freiherr von Langen, was placed first out of 102 entries at the international competition in Rome. This same horse when ridden by Duke Hohenau also won the 1926 German jumping derby against strong international competition.

At the end of the 1920s, the Hanover cavalry school formed a jumping stable. It was this stable which produced the German show-jumping teams up until 1940.

Draufgänger by Aldech, ridden by Freiherr von Langen.

Alchimist by Amalfi out of a mare by Colonus, at Aachen in 1937.

Olaf (born 1923), by Schwalk out of a mare by Köster.

Between 1928 and 1940, the German team won the Prix des Nations twenty-five times. Forty-one out of the 100 horses who competed during those twelve years were Hanoverians. Outstanding horses from this period were Alchimist by Amalfi, Derby by Island, Olaf by Schwalk, Oberst by Detektiv and Aland by Amalfi. Among the riders of these horses were such well-known names as Brinckmann, E. and K. Hasse, Momm, von Barnekow, von Nagel and Weidemann.

Competition horses since 1945

At the end of the war, in 1945, horse sports began to spread to the rural community and local, rural shows began to make an appearance. On the instigation of the Hanoverian breed society, the *Vorläufiger Ausschuss für Pferdeleistungsprüfungen* (Preliminary Board for Horse Performance Tests and Competitions) was set up in 1947. This was a precursor of the *Kommission für Pferdeleistungsprüfungen* (Committee for Horse Performance Tests and Competitions). The *Landesreiterverband Niedersachsen* (Lower Saxony Riders' Association), established in 1948, did much to promote riding in the rural community. Countless internationally famous competition horses received their early training in rural riding centres and clubs.

In 1950, the Hanoverian gelding Zigeunerbaron by Grunelius, ridden by Felix

Zigeunerbaron by Grunelius, ridden by Felix Bürkner, at Verden in 1950.

Bürkner, won the London dressage Grand Prix. This win was followed later in the 1950s by the great successes of the Duellant mare Doublette, ridden by Rosemarie Springer and Willi Schultheis. This mare won 100,000 DM in advanced dressage competitions, a figure which was unequalled by any German competition horse for a considerable time. Also of interest is the fact that she was bought through one of the early Verden auctions for 5000 DM.

In 1952, West German riders again began taking part in the Olympic Games and have continued to do so with considerable success. Hanoverian horses have featured prominently in this success as the following list of medal-winning Hanoverians shows.

1952 HELSINKI OLYMPICS: the West German three-day event team, with three Hanoverian horses, won the silver medal. These horses were Hubertus by Goldfisch I (Dr Willi Büsing), Trux von Kamax by Falkner III (Otto Rothe), and Dachs by Freddy II (Klaus Wagner).
1956 STOCKHOLM OLYMPICS: silver medal for the West German three-day event team with Trux von Kamax by Falkner III (Alfons Lütke-Westhues), who also won

Doublette by Duellant, ridden by Willi Schultheis.

Hubertus by Goldfisch I, ridden by Willi Büsing.

Trux von Kamax by Falkner III, ridden by D. Fösken at Luhmühlen in 1957.

the individual silver medal, Princess by Jubel I (Klaus Wagner) and Sissy by Fokker (Otto Rothe).

1960 ROME OLYMPICS: bronze medal for dressage won by Asbach by Anilin (Josef Neckermann); gold medal for show jumping won by the West German team, which included Ferdl by Ferdinand (Alwin Schockemöhle).

1964 TOKYO OLYMPICS: gold medal for the West German show-jumping team with Dozent by Deputant (Hermann Schridde) and Fidelitas by Dömitz (Hans Günter Winkler); gold medal for the West German dressage team with Dux by Duellant (Reiner Klimke); individual bronze medal in the three-day event with Donkosack by Dreikampf XX ridden by Fritz Ligges.

1968 MEXICO OLYMPICS: gold medal for the West German dressage team with Dux by Duellant (Reiner Klimke), who also won the individual bronze medal; bronze medal for the West German show-jumping team with the Hanoverians Enigk by Endspurt XX ridden by Hans Günter Winkler, Donald Rex by Durban (Alwin Schockemöhle), Dozent by Deputant (Hermann Schridde) and Simona by Weingeist (Hartwig Steenken).

1972 MUNICH OLYMPICS: gold medal for the West German show-jumping team with Simona by Weingeist (Hartwig Steenken) and Askan by Almhügel III (Paul Schockemöhle). Gold medal for the West German dressage team with Mehmed by

Simona by Weingeist, ridden by Hartwig Steenken.

Mehmed by Ferdinand, ridden by Dr Reiner Klimke.

Ferdinand (Reiner Klimke) and Liostro by Der Löwe XX ridden by Karin Schlüter. (Simona and Mehmed also won the 1974 World Championships in show jumping and dressage respectively.)

1976 MONTREAL OLYMPICS: gold medal for the West German dressage team with Woyczek by Wunsch II (Harry Boldt), who also won the individual silver medal, and Mehmed by Ferdinand (Reiner Klimke), who also won the individual bronze medal. Silver medal for the German show-jumping team with Warwick Rex by Wortschwall (Alwin Schockemöhle), who also won the individual gold, and Agent by Agram (Paul Schockemöhle).

In Montreal the Belgian show-jumping team won the bronze medal, riding Hanoverians or horses of Hanoverian extraction bred in Belgium. Of the twenty-five German-bred horses which competed in the various branches of equestrian sport at the Montreal Olympics, seventeen were Hanoverians. These seventeen horses were members of teams from ten different countries. Among the top horses there were more Hanoverians than any other breed, and the widespread international popularity of the Hanoverian as a top-class competition horse continued to flourish throughout the 1980s.

In 1979 there were about 16,500 registered mares in Hanover. Of all registered German warmblood mares, 29.5 per cent were Hanoverians. The fact that 68 per cent of the German horses which took part in the Montreal Olympics were Hanoverians shows both that Hanoverians are highly esteemed as top-level competition horses and that they are well suited to this role.

Hanoverian riding horses also distinguished themselves in the following competitions during the 1970s:

SLIBOWITZ by Servus out of a mare by Abhang II, ridden by Uwe Schulten-Baumer, was reserve champion in the World Dressage Championship in 1978.
MADRAS by Monaco out of a mare by Elegant, also ridden by Uwe Schulten-Baumer, won the 1981 European Dressage Championship.
DEISTER by Diskant out of a mare by Adlerschild XX, ridden by Paul Schockemöhle, won the 1981 European Show Jumping Championship.

(Opposite page)
Madras by Monaco, ridden by Dr Uwe Schulten-Baumer.

Deister by Diskant,
ridden by Paul
Schockemöhle.

EL PASO by Eindruck II out of a mare by Wachter, ridden by Paul Schockemöhle, won 323,000 DM, which was more than any other show jumper in West Germany at that time.

GLADSTONE by Götz out of a mare by Weingau, ridden by Hugo Simon, won the 1980 World Cup for Austria.

TIGRE by Widerhall out of a mare by Solarius XX, ridden by the late Caroline Bradley, helped win World Championship honours for England as a member of their 1978 show-jumping team.

(Opposite page)
Tigre by Widerhall, ridden by Caroline Bradley.

Gladstone by Götz,
ridden by Hugo Simon.

Every year about 12,000 to 13,000 new competition horses are registered with the German horse society, the *Deutsche Reiterliche Vereinigung (FN)*. In recent years about one-third of these have been Hanoverians, and the typical breakdown breed by breed can be shown by the figures for 1981.

No. registered	Breed	%
4033	Hanoverian	32.2
2313	Westphalian	18.5
917	Holstein	7.3
956	Oldenburg	7.6
787	Hessen	6.3
894	Trakehner	7.1
747	Rhineland	6.0
578	Bavarian	4.6
771	Baden-Württemberg	6.2
531	miscellaneous	4.2

Competition horse registrations 1981

The German horse society keeps a record of the total winnings of the progeny of individual stallions. For example, in 1981 the 120 most successful stallions had sired horses with winnings of between 157,127 DM and 1,353,407 DM. Of these sires, seventy-four (61.6 per cent) were either Hanoverians or Thoroughbreds which had stood at stud or were still standing at stud in the Hanoverian breeding zone. The top twenty of these sires were as follows:

1. Gotthard, born Hanover 1949   DM 1,353,407

	Stallion	Winnings
1.	Gotthard, born Hanover 1949	DM 1,353,407
2.	Ferdinand, born Hanover 1942	DM 1,053,858
3.	Der Löwe XX, born Röttgen Thoroughbred Stud 1944	DM 799,410
4.	Furioso II, born France 1965	DM 748,180
5.	Grande, born Hanover 1958	DM 713,245
6.	Ehrenschild, born Hanover 1956	DM 608,879
7.	Sender, born Hanover 1955	DM 571,381
8.	Domspatz, born Hanover 1952	DM 559,926
9.	Perser XX, born Mydlinghoven 1952	DM 532,004
10.	Ladykiller XX, born England 1961	DM 503,950
11.	Agram, born Hanover 1939	DM 490,209
12.	Servus, born Hanover 1961	DM 489,312
13.	Pik As XX, born Mydlinghoven 1949	DM 461,954
14.	Don Carlos, born Hanover 1962	DM 461,209
15.	Lugano I, born Hanover 1954	DM 444,369
16.	Weingau, born Hanover 1954	DM 437,255
17.	Angelo XX, born Westphalia 1962	DM 422,959
18.	Absatz, born Hanover 1960	DM 417,659
19.	Paradox I, born Westphalia 1964	DM 408,162
20.	Diskant, born Hanover 1957	DM 398,739

Apart from the stallions Furioso II (Selle Français graded into the Hanoverian and Oldenburg stud books), Ladykiller XX (graded into the Holstein stud book), Angelo XX (graded into the Westphalian stud book), and Paradox I (Westphalian), all these sires are Hanoverians or Thoroughbreds which stood at stud in the Hanover zone. This system of evaluating stallions according to the winnings of their progeny is similar to that in use for Thoroughbred racehorse sires, though it does not give such a clear picture as for racehorses since with warmblood sports there are more factors involved than just speed.

11 Recent developments

Modern breeding policy

The Hanoverian Society in West Germany is probably the best known of the present warmblood breeding organisations, chiefly because of its large numbers of registered stock, its excellent publicity and marketing techniques and the impressive results of the Hanoverian horse in the international competition world. As a breed, the Hanoverian is continually being developed to produce and maintain it as the modern type of riding horse suitable for today's market. A few years ago the name 'Hanoverian' was almost always associated with a big, powerful, elastic, but often quite plain horse more suited to a male rider than to a female one. Now, with the introduction of increasing amounts of Thoroughbred, Selle Français, Anglo-Arab and Trakehner blood, the modern Hanoverian is a more average-sized horse, with a better front and wither and more overall quality.

As has been mentioned in an earlier chapter, computer statistics play a very important role in West German breeding policy. Detailed records of every stallion, how many of his produce are registered as competition horses, what prize money they have won, and in what disciplines are all recorded on file. Such data as how many of his daughters have been awarded State Premiums as broodmares, or how many of his sons have become graded stallions are also on the computer, and all this information is made available to the general public. These statistics are important in establishing the most successful breeding combinations as well as determining the best stallions and sales prospects of the future. This system is of great use to the serious breeders and trends are easy to assess.

Performance testing for mares

The growing importance of statistics and reliable data in breeding, developing and marketing the Hanoverian has meant that the possibility of ridden performance testing for all mares has been discussed many times in the past, particularly as all State Premium mares have been required to complete a successful ridden test for some years. Recently, a system of longer ridden tests has been made available for a much wider selection of mares, and since 1988 the mare's ridden test has been held six or seven times a year at Verden. Each test lasts for eighteen days with a 'finishing exam' taking place on the final day.

The Verden auctions

Modern marketing of the Hanoverian horse has played an important role in the continued success of the breed in the 1980s. Breeders will only carry on as long as the sales returns are viable, and to encourage them the Hanoverian *Verband* organise a number of sales annually for riding horses, foals, broodmares and – since 1988 – yearlings. As has been the practice for a number of years, the stallions are sold at the Verden licensing show, both those having passed and those having failed coming forward before the prospective purchasers. Many of them are sold abroad or to other breed societies within West Germany. They then have to pass the grading standards required in their new homes. In Great Britain, for instance, the British Warm-Blood Society will not allow any stallions who have not successfully completed any part of the grading process they have undertaken to come forward for grading, whereas in Denmark only colts receiving marks in the top third of their licensing year will be eligible for inspection or grading for entry into the Danish Warmblood Breeding Stud Book. Buyers of potential stallions should therefore always ensure that they are aware of the requirements of the stud book into which they wish to enter their new purchase, before selecting an animal to buy.

New stallions of the 1980s

The modern Hanoverian up-dated its established lines in the 1980s with judiciously introduced new bloodlines, as well as importing a number of impressive young stallions who are starting to found new lines.

Bolero by Black Sky XX out of a Bleep XX mare was a relatively short-lived three-quarter Thoroughbred stallion who has made an enormous impact in recent years. He produced numerous champions, both at the stallion licensing and at the mare gradings, as well as at the National Riding Horse Championships. He also has graded sons in Denmark and the USA.

Woerman, from the Wohler line, died in 1989, but by that time his sons Wenzel, World Cup I, World Cup II and World Cup III were already making their mark in the breeding world, and their progeny is well sought after in breeding pedigrees.

Matcho X (by Pancho II), an Anglo-Arab imported from France for Celle, is as yet

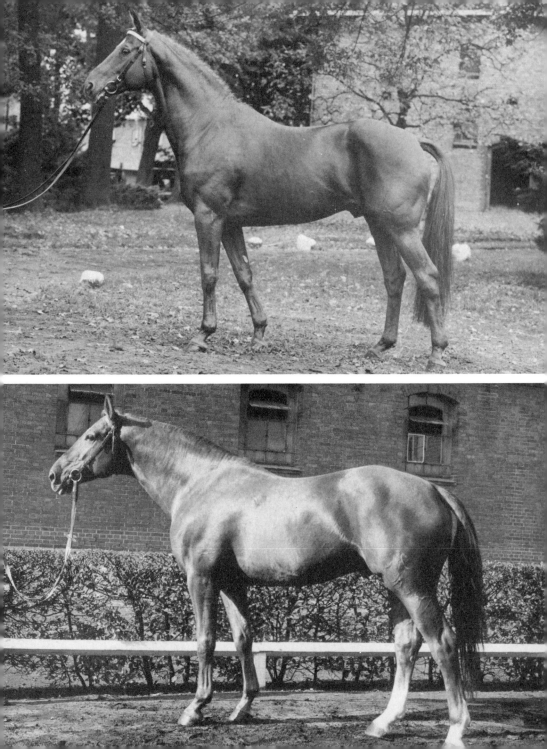

The French-bred Matcho X (by Pancho II X out of Timab de Fondelyn X by Karikal IV X), an Anglo-Arab stallion graded by the Hanoverian *Verband* in 1982, who is already making his name, particularly as a sire of graded sons and State Premium mares. (*Photo:* © *Werner Ernst*)

(Opposite page)
Bolero (by Black Sky XX out of Baronesse by Bleep XX), a sadly short-lived stallion who made a powerful impact during his ten years at stud. (*Photo:* © *Werner Ernst*)

Woermann (by Wohler out of Mandat by Marabou XX), who after going to stud in 1974 made his name as a sire of stallions very quickly, having twenty-one graded sons by 1989. (*Photo:* © *Werner Ernst*)

rather young to have made a long-term impression in Hanoverian pedigrees, but his sons – including the 1988 stallion licensing champion Maurice (out of a Garibaldi II mare) – have certainly caught the eyes of the breeders. He also has a graded son out of a G-line mare standing in Denmark. The popularity of Matcho X reflects the enthusiasm for the French-bred sires of the 1970s such as Furioso II (by Furioso XX), who produced extremely well when crossed with Hanoverian mares, siring some very high money earners in competition. Other French imports, some of them purchased by respected stallion owners, include Bonsoir, Quo Vadis, Zeus and Vertisas X, who should all play a major role in the new generation of Hanoverians in the 1990s.

Other young stallions who look likely to make an impact include the Thoroughbreds Prince Orac XX by Good Times XX and Nuegen XX by Hardicanute XX, the Landgraf I son Landfurst and the two Argentan sons Al Capone and Archipel. Finally, the young sire Wanderer (by Wagner out of a Shogun XX mare) already has three sons selected for Celle and looks sure to be an important line for the future.

Hanoverian breeding in Great Britain

Great Britain has been slow to embrace a system of inspection, statistics and performance results in breeding a pedigree horse for competition. A few warmblood stallions were imported from abroad in the 1960s and their influence can mainly be seen in the Maple Duellist (by Duellant) bloodline started by the Hon. Mrs J. Kidd at the Maple Stud. There are a number of excellent dressage horses competing today who descend from this line. Unfortunately, although Ministry of Agriculture stallion licensing was still in existence at that time, there was no official organisation set up to issue registration or pedigree papers and certainly no formal system of inspection or grading offered by any specialist breed society. This has made it difficult to trace the ancestry of many of the Hanoverian crosses born in the country over the years. At present, Great Britain still has fewer warmblood sires at stud than many breeders and competition riders would wish, and it is still not possible to keep comprehensive records of their progeny, although progress has been made in starting such a scheme based on computer records.

Between 1980 and 1990 a number of Hanoverian stallions were imported, some of whom had been both licensed and successfully performance tested in West Germany. The Hanoverian *Verband* will brand and issue papers to the foals sired by these stallions, providing they are out of pedigree Hanoverian mares that are also graded and entered into the breeding stud books of the *Verband* in West Germany.

In addition, the British Warm-Blood Society (BWBS) now requires Hanoverian stallions imported into Britain to go through its own separate grading process and veterinary inspection before they can enter the British Warm-Blood Society stud book for breeding. Foals born in Britain must be sired by currently BWBS-graded and registered stallions to be eligible for BWBS registration and pedigree papers. The British Warm-Blood Society also supplies pedigree papers to breeders of eligible foals who do not wish to register them in West Germany, and for foals produced by graded sires out of mares graded in Britain rather than West Germany. (Such mares are often Thoroughbreds.) As has been mentioned earlier, no stallion that has failed a grading abroad is eligible to attend the British Warm-Blood Society stallion grading. Unfortunately, however, despite the efforts of the society, there are still a large number of Hanoverian stallions being used at stud in Britain who have not passed any grading, or indeed who may have actually failed a grading. These stallions often stand at very low stud fees and as yet there is no government ruling to prevent this.

There are quite a number of good bloodlines available in Great Britain. However, possibly because of the large number of light Thoroughbred mares in the country, most of the stallions are of the heavier type that found favour in West Germany a few years ago. This tends to make breeding the ideal type of modern Hanoverian somewhat difficult in Britain, particularly as putting two such different light and heavy types together is not always successful and can produce a rather unharmonious product. In addition, because of the limited number of Hanoverian breeding stock in the country, there are just not sufficient numbers of quality animals to give either the stallion owners a choice of mares, or the mare owners a choice of stallions. This is never a problem in West Germany where there is an extremely wide choice of stallions and mares available. Unfortunately, the tendency of British breeders to breed 'pure' Hanoverian, in a mistaken interpretation of European breeding practices, too often produces unsatisfactory results when the two individuals concerned are unsuited to each other. So while Britain now has both some excellent stallions and some excellent mares, they are often incompatible with each other in weight and type. In West Germany, on the other hand, each stallion station offers mare owners a selection of between two and seven sires from which to choose, so a plainish heavy mare can go to an elegant stallion, whilst a part-Thoroughbred mare could go back to a more substantial sire. In both cases an ideal middleweight, of average size, with quality and elastic movement is the goal, but this is achieved over several generations, rather than by mating opposites for a quick result.

The first West German registered and licensed Hanoverian stallion to be imported into Britain was Mr H. Rose's Wineberg by Winnetou. He is a sire who has produced well, and he is known for the success of his progeny in-hand and in ridden hunter classes. He is also beginning to be well represented in the dressage arena. He has proved himself to be an all-round sire, crossing well with the native Thoroughbred mares, yet not being too heavy for many Hanoverian mares. His bloodlines seem to produce an ideal modern competition animal, very well suited to today's market.

The famous G-line is represented by the two Grande line stallions, Bold Venture Stud's Guardian (by Garibaldi II) and Townhead Stud's Gymnast by Grenadier, and by Mr J. Barrington's Götz grandson Galvarno by Gigant. The Grande line stock can tend to be rather plain in type, and are often very substantial, having a considerable

Grande, by Graf out of StPrSt Duellfest by Duellant. The sire of over forty graded stallions and winners of a total of over 1 million DM in competitions under saddle in Germany alone, he was one of the outstanding G-line sire of the 1970s and 1980s. (*Photo: © Werner Ernst*)

aptitude for jumping. As the progeny of Gymnast and Guardian are just reaching competition age, future years will have to judge their worth as sires, although Galvarno is already making a name for himself as the sire of Gildernstern (out of a Thoroughbred mare by Firestreak), the reserve champion of the 1988 Masterlock Recruitment Potential Competition Horse Championship, which is the only European-style young riding horse competition organised in Britain.

Confusingly, Furze Hill Stud's grey stallion Galant (by Galan) is not from the best-known G-line (which hails from Goldfisch II), although his name begins with G. He is an interesting mixture, having a partbred Arab sire (hence the grey colour) and Wedekind (by Ferdinand) as his dam's sire. Wedekind has produced both dressage and show-jumping progeny, as well as being a prolific sire of licensed stallions. Another stallion with some Arab blood is Maple Courier (by Kurier, a part Anglo-Arab). Purchased in 1976 as a replacement for Maple Duellist, he produced some notable dressage horses including Cocum Eliab during his ten years at the Maple Stud. Unfortunately, he was sold when the stud was dispersed and since 1986 he has not stood at public stud.

Broadstone Stud's Demonstrator (by Dynamo out of a mare by Pik Bube) is one of the very few graded Hanoverian stallions to compete in dressage in Britain. Black and eye-catching, he has been working his way up under the English-based West German trainer Ferdi Eilberg. His progeny are still too young for serious ridden competition, but both his sire and his dam's sire have made their mark in West German statistics.

Mrs Eva Kirby's Akkord (Aperitif/Sender) came from the Hunnesrück Stud Farm and was purchased privately by his enthusiastic owner. His progeny are already doing well, and perhaps best known is Abrakadabra, who came third in the National Medium Dressage championships in 1988 under Jane Bartle Wilson. Akkord is also unique amongst the Hanoverian stallions in Britain in two ways: he is the only one to have been featured in the *100 Year Jubilee Hanoverian Stud Book* and he is the only one to have sired a champion stallion at a British Warm-Blood Society Stallion Grading, when his son Stonegrove Ace (out of a Mansingh XX mare) was successful in 1989.

Two older stallions, imported after standing a number of years abroad, are Wendepunkt (Wendekreis/Einglas), who is now owned by Capt. Peter Hall, and Mr Stephen Hobbs' Odysseus (Orbis XX/Dorilas). Wendepunkt is very well thought of in West Germany, where he originally stood at stud privately, but unfortunately prior to going to Capt. Hall he was not used much in Britain. Although he now has a

Akkord, by Aperitif, the only British-based licensed Hanoverian stallion to be featured in the *100 Year Jubilee Hanoverian Stud Book*.

son Wenditor (born 1985 out of a Windsor mare) who is graded with the British Warm-Blood Society, a graded son in Belgium and a graded son at Celle, he is still only being used very lightly at stud, partly because of his age. Odysseus first stood at stud in West Germany, and then went to Denmark where he competed successfully as a Grade A show jumper before being sold to the UK in 1981, and has proved to be a popular sire for a wide variety of mares.

Finally, there were two Lugano descendants in Britain by the end of the 1980s: Leuchtfeuer (by Leutnant) and the young stallion Limbo (Lanthan/Woermann). Both are the more modern sires in type and seem to do well on a wide variety of mare

(Opposite page)
Odysseus, by Orbis XX, who has stood at stud in both Denmark and Great Britain since being exported from Germany, and has also competed in Puissance classes.

material, particularly in the case of Limbo who has the very good mother line of Woermann in his pedigree.

As well as the Hanoverian *Verband* licensed horses mentioned above, there are numerous other stallions graded with the British Warm-Blood Society who were imported from West Germany prior to their licensing, or who carry a large percentage of Hanoverian blood but were imported from countries outside West Germany. This group includes such important sires as the Durfee Stud's Danish Warmblood Atlantus (Abglanz, Wohler and Der Löwe XX blood), who is already responsible for several top show jumpers including Byron, the Grand Prix winner at Donauschingen for the USA, and Quanto, who is now in Japan; Warcolag Stud's British Warmblood Finale (by a Furioso II stallion out of a mare by Doktorand I); Cranswick Warm-Blood Stud's Akkurat (Akrobat/Sesam I), the sire of the good young dressage horse Aktress; and finally, Mrs Jane Walker's British Warm-Blood Society Stallion Grading Champion of 1986, the Hanoverian Domsberg (Damnatz/Akrobat) who was imported in utero from West Germany. Stallions such as these are therefore also helping to extend the influence of Hanoverian blood in the British competition horse to a significant degree.

Hanoverian breeding in North America

With the success of Hanoverian-bred stock in recent Olympic Games, particularly in Los Angeles where Metternich by Marmor competed for Mexico in dressage and Anklang by Adlerfarn II and the World Cup winner Aramis by Argentan both competed for Canada in dressage and show jumping respectively, North America has seen a staggering growth in the number of stallions and mares with Hanoverian blood at stud. Sadly, as has been the case with several breeding districts outside the mainland of Northern Europe, the all-important need to inspect and licence or grade breeding stock has sometimes been overlooked in the wish to meet a quickly expanding market for Hanoverian horses. This has meant that there has occasionally been a somewhat 'unharmonious' look to some of the animals foaled in Canada and the USA that are described by their owners as 'Hanoverian'. Strictly speaking the term 'Hanoverian' can only be used with reference to a horse with papers issued by the *Verband Hannoverischer Warmblutzüchter eV* or its officially recognised local representative – in this case the American Hanoverian Society (or AHS), who have recently begun to run German-style 100-day performance tests for American-bred Hanoverians with acceptable pedigrees and conformation. Other organisations in

North America do register and performance test Hanoverian stallions along with other breeds, and register the progeny of approved stallions and mares (most notably the International Sporthorse Registry), but only in the case of the *Verband* and the AHS are 'Hanoverian' papers issued for recognised 'Hanoverian' foals.

The incredible growth in the breeding of Hanoverians and the use of Hanoverian stallions on Thoroughbred mares or mares of other warmblood breeds to produce a homebred competition horse in North America can best be illustrated by a few statistics. Each year in December the American magazine *Chronicle of the Horse* publishes a stallion issue, which is widely acknowledged to be one of the best and most comprehensive guides to what is happening in the competition horse breeding world in Canada and the United States. Until the early 1980s a large percentage of the stallions featured were Thoroughbreds, and in 1984 only thirty-five Hanoverians were advertised as being at stud, with nineteen of these being licensed by the *Verband*. By 1985 the figure had risen to 59, by 1986 it was 112, by 1987 it had dropped slightly to 94 and by 1988 it was the most popular breed with 122 stallions advertised. Unfortunately, only about 75 per cent of these stallions have completed any form of grading procedure, for – as in Britain – there are no legal compulsory controls on stallion standards, but hopefully the increasingly discriminating mare owner's market will ensure that the poorer specimens are less and less patronised as time goes on. Statistics published in the official German magazine *Hannoversches Pferd* in February 1989 indicated that there were forty-four *Verband* licensed stallions at stud in the USA at that time, with a further sixteen based in Canada.

Although the enthusiasm of American breeders for the Hanoverian has meant that some rather dubious animals are at stud, it has also enabled some outstanding stallions to be imported because of the large number of mare owners willing to pay high stud fees for good bloodlines and a proven record. In addition, chilled semen is very popular because the vast distances which can prove a hindrance to having a choice of bloodlines available cease to be a problem, and distance becomes no object in choosing a stallion. Probably the most important of the senior stallions is Thornbrook Farm's DLG *Seiger* stallion (i.e. champion at the DLG show) Dirk (Duft II/Senator). The sire of four graded stallions and a number of state premium mares, his progeny have won nearly DM 200,000 in competition. His stablemates at Thornbrook Farms are Wishing Well (Werther/Dagobert) and Winchester (Winnetou/Sender). Another well-known stallion is the Winterwood based Grundstein (Graphit/Sermon), who is the leading sire of all breeds for dressage horses born in West Germany in 1978 and has thirteen fully licensed sons at stud. V. E. Batchelder's

Gastronom (by Gazal out of StPrSt Constanze by Ceylon) was exported to the USA in 1983, where he is a popular sire amongst competition horse breeders. (*Photo:* © *Werner Ernst*)

(Opposite page)
Dirk (by Duft II out of Semester by Senator), one of the top Hanoverian sires exported to the USA after a successful stud career in West Germany, where he left three graded sons. (*Photo:* © *Werner Ernst*)

Grundstein (by Graphit out of a mare by Sermon), a noted sire of both graded stallions and dressage horses who has stood at stud for several years in the USA. (*Photo:* © *Werner Ernst*)

125

Gazal son Gastronom is also proving popular and left a Celle-based stallion, Gaspano (out of a Dolentino mare), behind him before he departed for the New World. Gaspano followed his sire to the USA recently and is now based in Texas.

The top stallion at the 1980 licensing also found his way to the USA. Elektron (Einblick/Winnetou), who is based at Cinema Farms, has competed in show jumping in his new home and is one of the few stallions of this line at stud in North America.

G-line stallions at stud in North America include November Hill Farm's Glanzpunkt (Gaston/Steppenwolf) and the Grande son Grandduell, who is out of a Duellant mare.

Finally, and certainly deserving a special mention, is Aktuell (Absatz/Valentino), recently imported into the USA with an outstanding reputation as a sire in West Germany.

With modern transport systems and modern technology, much American breeding involves the use of either chilled or frozen semen, and in some cases embryo transplant as well. The wealth of bloodlines thus available, plus the possibility of importing semen from internationally renowned sires, ensures that the choice offered to North American breeders is as comprehensive as possible, and this should be a good foundation on which to build in the future.

Although it is obviously not desirable to have multiple embryos from one mating, and the produce of such techniques might not be registerable with the Hanoverian *Verband* (who have also shown a certain reluctance to allow artificial insemination using semen from stallions not permanently based in West Germany), it is not felt that the possibility of the over-use of one stallion to the exclusion of all others is likely. This is because not only is a wide choice of stallions available, but also the number of straws of semen and the way they are distributed are closely controlled by all concerned.

The Hanoverian competition horse worldwide

By the end of the 1980s there were over eighty Hanoverian stallions registered and licensed in West Germany but who were standing outside the Federal Republic. The breakdown of figures (see table opposite) provides an interesting comparison with the export figures of yesteryear. However, the immense influence of the Hanoverian horse worldwide does not just rest on its prepotent breeding characteristics. For riders in many countries that do not have their own indigenous, or organised, warmblood breeding system, or where the demand for top-class competition horses

Country	No. of licensed Hanoverian stallions at stud
Australia	3
Brazil	1
Canada	16
Great Britain	10
Luxemburg	1
Mexico	1
Namibia	3
The Netherlands	1
New Zealand	2
South Africa	2
Switzerland	1
United States of America	44
Yugoslavia	2
Total	87

Licensed stallions worldwide, 1989

outstrips the supply of locally available stock, a trip to West Germany to buy a Hanoverian can be one answer to many of their problems. The importance of this worldwide market continued to grow throughout the 1980s despite the strength of the Deutschmark, and can be best shown in the following list of Hanoverian horses competing in the 1984 and 1988 Olympic Games for countries other than West Germany.

AUSTRIA 1984: Acapulco by Absatz (dressage)
1988: Gipsy Lady by Gardestern (show jumping)
AUSTRALIA 1988: Furst Z by Furst Ferdinand (show jumping); Whisper Grey by Widerhall (show jumping)
BRAZIL 1988: Wendy by Wedekind (show jumping)
CANADA 1984: Anklang by Adlerfarn II (dressage); Aramis by Argentan (show jumping)

1988: Dynasty by Darling (dressage)

EGYPT 1988: Tric Trac by Securius (show jumping)

FINLAND 1988: Pakistan by Partisan (dressage)

JAPAN 1984: Medina by Matrose (dressage)

1988: Medina by Matrose (dressage)

MEXICO 1984: Metternich by Marmor (dressage)

THE NETHERLANDS 1988: Doreenlasilla by Diskus (show jumping)

NEW ZEALAND 1988: Bago by Winnebago (show jumping)

SOUTH KOREA 1988: Lugana by Lugano II (dressage)

SPAIN 1984: Feinschnitt Z by Wendekreis (show jumping)

1988: Rex the Blacky by Ortwin (show jumping)

SWITZERLAND 1988: Diners Dollar Girl by Dynamo (show jumping); Shandor by Winnetou (show jumping)

UNITED STATES OF AMERICA 1988: The Natural by Diskus (show jumping); Federlicht by Federgeist (dressage)

A total of no fewer than fourteen different countries represented by twenty-one different horses in just two Olympic Games! It is doubtful if any other breed has achieved this consistency at the highest level over a number of years, and these figures are a true testimony of the continuing success of the Hanoverian breed throughout the world.

Conclusion

The warmblood horse bred in Hanover has been a breed in its own right for over 120 years. Hanover is now the largest organised riding horse breeding zone in Europe.

From the outset, Hanoverian breeders have worked in close liaison with the breeding authorities to produce a horse which would sell. For 100 years they managed to satisfy the need for a tough performance horse for the army as well as the demand for an honest horse with substance for use on the farm. Since the English Thoroughbred arrived on the continent, this has been used to a greater or lesser extent (depending on the requirements of the period) as a positive influence, and Trakehner and Arab blood has also been used in moderation for up-grading purposes.

The boom in equestrian sport which has taken place since the mid 1960s both in Europe and overseas has enabled the talented, versatile Hanoverian to become established both at stud and in the competition arena beyond the boundaries of its breeding zone and outside Germany.

Bibliography

Gramatzki, Fritz. *Handbuch Pferde*, Osnabrück, 1977

Köhler, Hans Joachim. *Hannovers edles Warmblut*, Hamburg–Munich–Neuhaus (Oste), 1949

Köhler, Hans Joachim. *Hannoversche Pferde: Geschichte, Zucht, Erfolge*, Lucerne, 1977

Lehndorff, Siegfried (Graf von). *Ein Leben mit Pferden*, Berlin, 1943

Rau, Gustav. *Die Not der deutschen Pferdezucht*, Stuttgart, 1907

Rau, Gustav. *Die deutschen Pferdezuchten*, Stuttgart, 1911

Rau, Gustav. *Die wichtigsten Blutströme in der hannoverschen Pferdezucht*, Berlin, 1914

Schlie, Arnold and Hans Löwe. *Der Hannoveraner*, Munich, 1975

Schöttler, Friedrich. *Das hannoversche Pferd*, Hanover, 1925

Stapenhorst, Hans. *200 Jahre Landgestüt Celle*, Celle, 1935

Stegen, Hermann. *Die Zucht des hannoverschen Pferdes*, Hanover, 1934

Stenglin, Christian Freiherr von. *Das Landgestüt Celle und die hannoversche Zucht*, Celle 1959

Unger, Wolfgang von. *Die Ahnen des Hannoveraners*, Hanover, 1928

Viergutz, Gerhard. *Hengstbuch der deutschen Staatsgestüte*, vol. 1, *Landgestüt Celle und Osnabrück*, Hanover, 1939

Regional archives at Celle

Breeding Division Year Book 1981, German National Equestrian Federation, Warendorf

Stud books and archives of the *Verband Hannoverscher Warmblutzüchter*

Hannoversches Pferd magazine, various issues. (English-speaking members of the Hanoverian *Verband* now receive a twice-yearly English-language version of abstracts of the contents of this magazine)

Index of horses' names

Numbers in italics refer to illustrations.

132

133